WHAT IF I HAD A FATHER?

MIKE | DEAN

HUSBAND. **FATHER.** PASTOR. AUTHOR.
www.**deanbooks**.com

What If I Had a Father?

The Man I Never Knew

Mike Dean

To my mom, the late Sandra Lee Dean, my brother, the late Rodney S. Spencer Dean, the late Pastor Clarence Caldwell, and my beloved best friend, the late Maurice D. Randle.

"It don't do good to know, if you don't do good with what you know…"

~Clarence Caldwell

CONTENTS

ACKNOWLEDGMENTS

I would like to express my gratitude to the many people who saw me through this book: to all those who provided support, talked things over, read, wrote, offered comments, allowed me to quote their remarks and assisted in the editing, proofreading and design.

Above all I want to thank my wife, Val, my kids and the rest of my family (Dean and Davis), friends and mentors, who prayed, supported and encouraged me in spite of all the time it took me away from them. It was a long and difficult journey for them.

I would like to thank the YouthBuild movement for providing me with top-notch training and endless opportunities. I have many people throughout the United States and abroad that I can call my brothers and sisters because of you.

I would like to thank Jamie Turner and Erin Speicher, for helping me in the process of selection and editing when

I needed them the most. Thanks to my Power City Church family who encouraged me.

Last but not least: I thank my Lord and Savior Jesus Christ for changing my life and making me the man I've become, and using so many people along the way.

Thank you.

FOREWORD

DOROTHY STONEMAN

Mike Dean tells the story of his childhood with an open heart, a questioning mind, a poetic spirit, and deep empathy and compassion for everyone he has encountered. His perspective on the highs and the lows, the horrible experiences he personally lived through on the one hand, and the loving kindness of some of his family members on the other hand, is gentle in its understanding of humanity. He searches for answers to the unknown, and accepts that he will never know, even as he takes and communicates important lessons from the real experiences he had.

He dramatically communicates the impact of fatherlessness, the damage of physical and sexual abuse, and painful poverty. He equally as powerfully shares the importance of every act of kindness and every caring relationship a young child experiences growing up. Mike's book should inspire all fathers to play a bigger and more conscious role in their children's lives. It should inspire every mentor, every potential mentor, every teacher and counselor, to know that their roles as surrogate parents are sacred and land deep in the hearts of every child or young man to whom they give their caring attention. It should inspire every family member to reach out to the suffering children of less fortunate brothers and sisters or nieces and nephews who are eager for a bit of hope. It should inspire every convict to read many books and "come out of prison smarter."

Mike writes clearly as a young man who lacked a father. But the lessons of his book apply also to young women who suffer different challenges, but need the love of family members and others just as much, and who especially need help managing the impact of sexual abuse, as did Mike's mother.

Mike Dean survived. He took every possible lesson from his experience. Now, as an adult, as a husband and father of five, as a pastor, and the Director of a YouthBuild program deliberately benefitting young men like himself, he personifies the absolute best of everything he encountered. This fact is a testament to the resilience of the human spirit and the power of love.

I met Mike nearly twenty years ago, when he first stepped up as a leader in his YouthBuild Columbus program. He was sent to Orlando, Florida to represent his program. He was elected to the YouthBuild National Alumni Council. He became Vice President, and finally, after his dedicated and loving service as an officer of that Council for two years, he was elected President of the YouthBuild National Alumni Council.

Every step of the way on this leadership journey, Mike exuded a receptive and a generous spirit of loving kindness. He was always open to seeing, internalizing, and expressing the best values that would benefit humanity. He was a unifier, a giver. How did this happen? Where did his goodness come from? Is it an inherent human quality? Did he get it from his Aunt Phil? From his Uncle Shug? From the wonderful year he spent as a seven-year-old child in North Carolina with his Uncle Shug's family? Was there something about his mother and his father that laid the groundwork invisibly despite their more painful faults? Was it from his mother who loved her children enough to fight tooth and nail for them to have at least a mattress to sleep on and some food to eat even through her own addictions? Was it the extended family that somehow held together a little bit no matter how distressed the lives of some of its members?

When Mike Dean found his way to YouthBuild, he was like thousands of other young men and women. He had experienced incredible pain and loss, endless traumatic and horrifying moments, unbelievable obstacles. Yet his heart was open as he sought for hope, for safety, for a community and family that would be consistently kind and caring. When he found it, he led it. He now speaks for literally millions of young men and women who have had similar experiences, and are seeking a way out and up.

He continues to lead, to teach, to love. He is the first YouthBuild graduate to write a book, the first to become a pastor with his own church, and one of the first to have his own construction business. He is among the first half-dozen graduates to become the director of a YouthBuild program in his own community, to give back what he received to large numbers of young men and women. His family is thriving, his YouthBuild program doing immeasurable good for hundreds of young people.

Mike summarizes his lessons learned with such force and clarity. They will be excellent guides to anyone who takes them seriously. His wisdom reverberates with a sense of truth for all people. He didn't make it up. He didn't learn it secondhand. He learned it from the true trials and tribulations of surviving poverty and abuse with a learning mind and a loving soul coupled with a few people available to welcome him at critical moments with love and respect. Let us all be inspired at the resilience of the human spirit, especially a spirit like Mike Dean's, when there are visible examples of goodness and hope anywhere in the environment. Let us all make it our business to provide such examples for all children everywhere.

Mike also makes important observations about how the

economic and criminal justice systems perpetuate injustice and poverty. He names some actions that should be taken to change this.

His book is both a pleasure to read, and worth reading for its inspiration and its illumination of the reality faced by millions of Americans living in poverty. It highlights the moral imperative to eliminate those destructive conditions if young people are to grow up safe and thrive in America.

Many thanks to Mike Dean for taking the best from everything and giving his best to everyone. He is a gift for which we are grateful.

-Dorothy Stoneman
Founder and CEO, YouthBuild USA, Inc.

INTRODUCTION

"Fathers make a deposit in you through which you can make a withdrawal the rest of your life."
~TD Jakes

In your lifetime there are two significant people who play the biggest role in shaping who you become: your mother and father. As you journey with me through my book, *What If I Had a Father? The Man I Never Knew,* I want you to think about all of the moments in your life when you truly needed your father. Was he, or was he not there for you? If he wasn't there, how did you feel in those moments without the strong support of the man you needed most?

Fatherlessness is one of the most swept under-the-rug issues facing society today, and it concerns me that it has become such a widely accepted paradigm. Truth be told, fathers are more important than the accepted way of thinking, which has permeated our communities. While you journey with me through *What If I Had a Father?,* I will do my best to show you why it is so important for fathers to be actively engaged in the lives of their children.

Another concern about "accepted fatherlessness" is that it has become a learned behavior for all involved parties. It has patterned itself throughout this generation. Let me make myself clear– fatherlessness has not only been accepted, but often, it is something that is expected.

I must say this at the onset of this book: I will not pull any punches. I want to encourage everyone whose father was absent emotionally or physically (or both).

WHAT HAPPENED?

Did he die defending your country? Did your father die at an early age? Did your father die of a terminal illness? Did you and your family have to watch him wither away like a tree losing its leaves during the fall season? Did your father go to prison for a long time, missing out on your entire childhood? The key point is this: no matter how horrific the situation was, it did not negate the fact that you still needed him.

He could have been abusive to your mother. He could have been a bank robber or drug dealer. Did he own his own business? Maybe he was a college professor. Maybe he was a rocket scientist. Or maybe he was a factory worker.

Maybe he committed suicide. Maybe he suffered injury from a crippling automobile accident. Maybe he worked as a computer engineer for a major software company. Maybe he was a celebrity. Or maybe instead of being there for you during your time of need, he was chasing dreams. Maybe he was a pastor so engulfed in the work of the Lord that he left you on the back burner. Maybe he was on the run or was hiding in a witness protection program. Maybe he doesn't even know that you were born.

No matter how old you are, there's something in the soul of your soul that cries out for the love and affirmation of your father. No matter how tough you may consider yourself, fatherlessness affects you in a way nothing else can. This is hard to talk about. "Fatherlessness" is not a hot topic in barbershops and beauty salons. For many people, however, just mentioning the topic is devastating. But the same questions reside: What happened? Why couldn't I have a father?

Trust and believe that I understand some fathers tried their best. I'm here to encourage these men to hold on, be strong, and never give up on their children. At the same time, I wish that absent fathers would realize the magnitude of their power in their children's lives.

I have a hard task; some may believe it's an impossible task. But it is only when we learn from our past that we can open up our future. We need to press on and pray for this generation that has been forgotten. I believe through the inspiration of this book, families will reunite. In the meantime, there will be a process deep down in the consciousness of individuals who have been abandoned by their fathers.

To those reading this book who have never suffered from abandonment of their father or mother, this book is still for you. Why? In order to create a healthier society, we must understand each other's path. Why? Many people do not understand how it feels to not know their father, and with that comes the mysteries that cloud your mind with wonder.

This is an opportunity to deliver not only a book, but a message to society using some of my personal experiences coupled with those of others. It is my hope that this book will hit home for millions upon millions of people who have been affected by fatherlessness. I will do my best, not only to paint a clear picture of these effects, but also to provide solutions for reconnection, especially for those who have the opportunity to reconnect with each other.

FATHERLESS CHILD

"When a father gives to his son, both laugh;
when a son gives to his father, both cry."
~William Shakespeare

As a child, I used to wonder why everyone around me knew their dads, but that wasn't the case for me. I never thought it was unrealistic or unreasonable to have a relationship with my father. The father-sized void in my life was a gaping hole tearing away at me, and at times the pain was unbearable. What made it even more frustrating was that I didn't know where to look for him. I didn't know who I should approach to get answers. In fact, I didn't even know where to start.

I was on a quest.

I wanted to know my dad because I felt like I was missing out on how life was "supposed to be." But at the same time, I wondered if my quest was in vain. I was on a quest to find someone who should have been there all along. No child should have to grow up without a father. I had high hopes of being able to legitimately call my biological father "dad," but it seemed all I could focus on was all the times that "should have been."

Although I had felt that my life was a mystery waiting to be solved, I knew with all of my heart things would end up getting better. I don't know a lot, but what I do know is that everyone who has ever been born has to have had a father. That was one of the few things that wasn't a mystery to me. Instead, the mystery was more about trying to find out who I was.

Trust and believe that life went on for me. I didn't think about my father or my quest all the time, but when I did a part of me always felt lost. I soon realized that time can be a friend or an enemy.

THE TREE THAT WITHERS

I often wondered if I had siblings or other family members I never met because of the absence of my father. How can we continue to grow as a family if we don't have the opportunity to meet all of our branches? Branches grow through affirmation, just like relationships. Once a person is affirmed then he or she is accepted. But I imagine that many branches from my family tree were missing, all because one very significant branch was missing. Yet, that "father" branch was unwilling to make the connections to allow for family growth.

I thought about this family growth recently when my wife and I kept my nephew Marvin (Mar-Mar) for a few days. He was about four months old at the time, and my wife and I had a blast! He's a baby, how could we not? I did all I could do to see him laugh and smile as I tickled him on his feet and under his arms. I made goofy sounds over and over like goo-goo, ga-ga and goo-chi-goo-chi-goo as I played with him. When I wanted his attention, I'd grab my car keys, or something that made some type of strange noise, and jingle them in his face. He was totally mesmerized and fully interested in my keys, trying to reach out and clasp them to the best of his ability. They'd slip out of his fingertips and he'd try again, determined not to let the keys out of his sight. Everything about him was pure. We were there to change his diaper as needed, feed him a lukewarm bottle of milk, and then pat him on the back until he burped. I noticed that his life experience was very limited, especially since he found joy just in rubbing my face and feeling the scruffiness of my unshaven facial hair.

At four months old, Mar-Mar was amused by the simplest things. He didn't need to go to the county fair or go fishing. He wasn't looking for any gifts under the Christmas tree. He had no complaints. He wasn't asking for a porterhouse steak from the best steakhouse in town. He didn't want to go see the latest movie, and he wasn't looking for any advice. All he wanted was to feel the love and care of those who surrounded him. In return, he naturally showed his love through his cute dimples as he laughed and smiled, or by resting in my arms when he was tired and ready to take a nap. The illustration I just described is something that many fathers have missed out on for one reason or another. The sad part is that right now at this very moment, an absent father is missing out on his own child's precious demonstration of pure love.

DADDY YOU CALLED HIM

Let's be real, some people have missing branches on their trees because those branches were ripped off suddenly. These are people who, at an early age, suffered the death of their father. It is truly a tragedy to lose a father who once was involved and engaged in your life. The involved father was at the hospital when you were born. Your first words were da-da, because his presence was felt. He kissed you on your forehead and told you he loved you. His tight, gripping hug left the sweet-smelling scent of his favorite cologne in your nostrils for hours.

He inspired you to take your first step. He was up with

you all night while you were teething. He taught you how to tie your shoes. He did not withhold from correcting you when you needed to be disciplined. When you broke your leg, he was first at the hospital. He took the training wheels off of your bicycle because he knew you didn't need them anymore.

He was your biggest fan when you played in the pee-wee football league. In fact, he shouted and cheered when you scored your first touchdown as if your pee-wee team was his favorite pro team and you were winning the Super Bowl. He came to your cheerleading competitions and recitals, and he sat with you in your class during your first day of preschool. He brought gifts and cupcakes to your kindergarten class on your birthday. He was there for you! He wasn't ashamed of you! He even named you! He never, ever neglected a moment to shower his love toward you. *"Daddy,"* you called him.

Boom! Then one day he was gone from the face of the earth as a result of some terminal illness, murder, suicide or accident. Suddenly, you had only memories of the times you shared with him.

Sometimes you think back and you remember when he had to spank you for acting out in school, or when he punished you for not doing your daily chores on time. But since he passed, even the bad times don't seem so bad. You may be reading this and thinking to yourself, "I miss my dad."

Those are real feelings. While you hold those memories in your heart, I imagine that your thoughts grapple and twist, wondering how life would be if he had survived that illness, that accident or that tragedy.

So, the challenge for you then becomes how to deal with the varying and collective thoughts of the could'ves, would'ves, and should'ves. You may even wrestle with guilt inside yourself. You may have thoughts of regret: "I wish I could take back what I said to him before he passed. I could have behaved better in school. I should have completed my chores in a timely manner. I could have been a better son (or daughter).

"Why?! Why did my daddy die?! Why did God take him away from me?! Why?! I needed more time with him, I need him! I need you, Daddy!

"I have a boyfriend that I'm not sure about, Daddy. I'm trying to use what you taught me, but I wasn't giving you my undivided attention when you were here! What was it you told me to watch out for with boys again? Daddy, I need you! Daddy, I'm stuck! I'm confused! I'm hurt! The pain is irrefutable. My right has become my left and my left has become my right. My ups have become my downs and my downs have become my ups. Daddy, if you can help me, and I hope you can, please forgive me! I hope you are like an angel, giving me little signs letting me know that you are watching over me. God, if you let my daddy come back, I promise to do right!

"If he were here I would at least receive some type of comfort to deal with my issues. Daddy, can you hear me?"

If you have experienced this kind of dialogue with God, no doubt you have also experienced tears flooding your eyes like the great flood in the days of Noah. Dealing with the death of a loved one is something that is hard to talk about. It takes time to recover. My thoughts and prayers are with anyone who has lost a parent. My hope is that you have a strong support system and that you can be transparent to someone about your real feelings. And when you are having a moment, let it out. The pain can eat you alive, and if you don't deal with the hole in your soul, then the pain remains.

One way I dealt with my own feelings is by escaping through sitcoms. Back in the 80s and 90s I let my imagination run wild with fantasy as I faithfully watched *The Wonder Years*, *MacGyver*, *Martin*, *Fresh Prince of Bel-Air*, *Doogie Howser*, *Hangin' with Mr. Cooper*, *Mama's Family*, *Family Matters*, *Married with Children*, *Rosanne* and *Saved by the Bell*.

But *The Cosby Show* stands out the most for me. That show had a great cast and it always seemed to put my mind at ease. Though it was fictional, the storylines had meaningful moral truths that often reminded me of the value of a father.

The Cosby Show had an interesting way of creating a standard of how a husband should love his wife and how a father should care for his children. The show touched on real-life issues that people dealt with every day. Every so often, Cliff and Clair Huxtable would have a disagreement, but by the end of the show they would figure out a way to communicate their feelings with each other. It seemed they could work through anything with the love and passion they shared for one another.

At times Cliff had to correct his children, but he was always fair. With every instance of discipline, Cliff taught his children something about life: he taught them that the decisions they made affected them. *The Cosby Show* also provided a distinct portrait of the importance of a father's support in his children's dreams. Even when Cliff and his son Theo didn't agree, there was still love and support–a strong bond between Father and son.

Cliff was clear and transparent about how he felt about the decisions his children were making, yet he peppered his feelings with guidance. There was an ease and grace in the way he handled his children. I admit that I often thought about what it would be like to have a father like him.

As much as I loved *The Cosby Show*, that kind of family dynamic wasn't at all my reality or the reality for most people. But the show captured my attention and played with my imagination. It definitely didn't hit home for me because it didn't show Cliff abusing Clair physically and/or mentally. It didn't show Cliff cheating on his wife. It didn't show Cliff locked up in prison. It didn't show Cliff without a job or struggling to care for his family.

But what if it did show those realities? Why didn't Theo watch his mom get beaten? Why weren't the Huxtables a blended family with Clair having had two children before she met Cliff? What if the storyline featured a Clair who married young and was widowed young after her first husband tragically died in a shootout? Maybe she loved her ex with all of her soul. Maybe he was her true and first love. Maybe when he was shot and killed, he whispered his last word to her: "Sorry." What if after experiencing great loss, she then found Cliff?

Why didn't the show allow Cliff to deal with a terminal illness like cancer? The audience never saw how Clair and the kids would have dealt with a tragic illness in their family, or what it would have been like for them to see their father connected to machines while eating through a tube. It was clear that the purpose of the show wasn't designed to illustrate those dysfunctions of life.

Having a father like Cliff Huxtable would have been amazing. But, realistically, you can't choose your parents, and for the sake of this writing, you can't choose your father. You can't choose the complexion of his skin. You can't choose his nationality. You can't choose his age. You have to work with whatever situation you were birthed into, like it or not. I'll even take it a step further: no human on the face of the earth has ever been able to choose his biological parents.

One can dream, though. If it were at all possible, I would choose for my father to have a combination of character traits from some of my heroes. He'd be a leader like Dr. Martin Luther King, Jr.; he'd be tough like Conan the Barbarian; he'd be smart like Albert Einstein; he'd have wisdom like Gandhi and he'd be there for me like Cliff Huxtable. And at the end of the day, that's the most important thing–all a child ever wants is for his father to be there for him.

It's like a two-year-old child lost in a mall. He wanders through a big space with no guidance, trying to get reconnected with his family. The child doesn't know where to go; all the child sees is strangers minding their own business. The pain of abandonment sets in and life becomes an instant whirlwind. For a small moment of time, that child feels a pain that is irrefutable. The crowded mind of a wounded soul is like being plunked right in the middle of Times Square during the New Year's Eve countdown, and being expected to find your own way out.

It's crazy to me how a man can be so heartless– how a man can just walk away, knowing deep down inside there is a poor little soul who yearns for the love of his father but will never receive it.

I will do my best to express in my own words the painful void deep down in the core of my mind. What happened to the heart of a father?

My Superhero

Most of my friends had fathers. Whenever I saw them share father-son moments with each other, I was reminded that I was fatherless. It didn't matter whether those times were good or bad. My friends knew who their fathers were. Their fathers didn't necessarily see them every day, which had to have been a pain all in itself. Most of those fathers had other families and would only come to visit their child on certain occasions or days. But my friends looked at their fathers like they were superheroes. Most of the time, the only thing their fathers couldn't do was fly. The way they tell it, their fathers could outswim a shark or outrun Flash Gordon. These fathers were even cooler than Michael Knight off of *Knight Rider*!

And even if those dads were no good, their kids still wanted to be like them. My friends looked up to their fathers even when they made promises they didn't keep. Those fathers had no idea the impact those broken promises had on their children.

As a child I tried to analyze the situation. I wondered how it felt when your hero let you down. How did it feel when your hero didn't honor his promise? What I noticed in my friends was that each time a father made a promise he didn't keep, it left a scar. Every time that happened, more scars ripped through their emotions. Even though some of my friends knew their fathers, I also wondered which was worse: knowing he was there and didn't care, or never seeing him show his face at all.

Some of my friends' fathers were forced out by women, who out of their own personal anger or vengeance, prevented them from having a healthy relationship with their children. Many times these same women used their children against their exes without knowing they actually were putting them on an emotional roller coaster. As a result, the children had to make mature decisions at a young age, and often may have felt pressured to choose sides or show loyalty to the parent they "loved the most." Yet, in the midst of all that chaos, at least those children had some type of relationship with their fathers.

Any type of relationship with a father had to be way better than not knowing him at all. They knew his voice, his walk, his car, his smell; they could spot him a mile away. Sometimes they looked like identical twins, and often the only difference would be the height.

I must admit, at times I was a little envious because I wanted that, too. Do I look like my dad? I don't know. Do I walk like my dad? I don't know. Do I sound like my dad? I don't know… I wanted a hug. I wanted to hear the words, "I love you, son." I wanted to know that when I needed him, I could call. I wanted to make him my superhero. But that wasn't the case for me, and sometimes it felt like I was being tortured.

I always wondered what my father was like. What type of personality did he have? Was he an introvert or an extrovert? How did he interact with his family? How did he interact with his peers? Was he the life of the party? Was he the quiet guy sitting on the wall, afraid to dance because he didn't have any moves?

How did he do in school? Did he have good study habits? Did he like to read? If he liked to read, what types of books did he enjoy? Did he like fiction, or non-fiction? Did he like novels or mysteries?

What was his favorite color? What were his political views? Was he democrat or republican? What type of car did he drive? Where did he like to shop? Did he like sports? Would he have helped coach my team? Or would he have cheered on the sidelines and encouraged me from there?

How did my grandparents treat him? How was his childhood? Was he a bully or did he get bullied? Did he ever ride in a plane? Did he ever ride a horse? Could he climb a mountain? Was he quick-tempered or short-tempered? Could he swim? I wanted so desperately to know my father–to know everything about him.

I could only imagine what having a father was like by looking at the fathers of my family and my friends. I imagined my ideal "Dr. Martin Luther King, Jr.-Conan-Einstein-Gandhi-Cliff Huxtable" father getting more and more excited in anticipation of my birth. I could only imagine the countless conversations with my mother about my future, my sports career and my spiritual values. But most of all, I imagined his excitement over how much his baby would act like him and how I would go along with him wherever he went.

But none of that was reality. To my father, I didn't exist. It was like I did something wrong to hurt him even before I was born.

Just like Mar-Mar, a baby doesn't care about rich, poor, color, height, weight, or what his father looks like. All any baby wants is to be loved. And while that also has been true for me, even into adulthood, the reality is this: things happened in my life that were beyond my control.

That reminds me of the movie, *The Pursuit of Happyness*. Will Smith and his own son, Jaden, star in this film inspired by the true story of Chris Gardner. Will plays "Chris," a San Francisco salesman, struggling to build a future for himself, and Jaden plays his five-year-old son, "Christopher."

Chris's girlfriend walks out, leaving him to raise little Christopher on his own. Living off of high hopes and self-determination of one day becoming a successful stockbroker, Chris earned an unpaid internship in a stockbroker-training program. But in the meantime, Chris and his son are evicted from their apartment, having no choice but to sleep on the streets. Together, Chris and his son did what they had to do in order to survive.

What touched me the most was when Chris looked at his son every day and gained the strength he needed with a "no matter what" mentality.

Christopher never gave up on his father, either. In fact, his father was his hero. One night, Chris and his son had to sleep in a public restroom at a subway station. All night, people tried to get in to use the restroom, but Chris locked the door and blocked it with his body just to be able to give his son a good night's sleep. That is the picture of a true hero, a hero even greater than the Spiderman toy little Christopher carried with him everywhere. And when Chris told his son a bedtime story while sitting on the floor of the subway restroom, he provided the same comfort of sleeping in the best bed that money could buy.

It didn't matter to Christopher that his father had no job; it didn't matter what color he was; and it didn't matter where they ate. All that mattered was that he and his father were together.

I know for a fact that the movie *The Pursuit of Happyness* didn't tell the entire story of their struggles. The visual that was created for this powerful masterpiece tells of the love a father has for his son, and the love the son has for his father. They didn't let anything come between them.

As I thought about this film, I processed the strong father-son connection between Chris and little Christopher. I also thought about my own father.

Without the son, would the father have been as determined to make it? Without the father, would the son ever have a chance to make it?

What if both parents walked out on that child?

Was my dad determined to make it without me?

What made my dad leave?

When a father is present in his child's life, that child's first spoken word is often, "Da-da." Those two syllables mean so much. They mean, "I know who you are. I know your voice. I recognize your scent." But most of all, "Da-da" means "I love you."

I never uttered the word "Da-da" because he wasn't there for me to know his voice or his scent. I was deprived of saying the simplest phrase in the world: "Da-da"! What did I do for that security to be withheld from me? I didn't ask to be here, so why me?

It would have been nice to have my father's input and perspective on life. He not only would have challenged me, but he could have sharpened my skillset. He could have given me direction and helped to create a level of focus. Of course, I learned to challenge myself, to look to God for direction and to create my own level of focus. But there are just some things a child learns best through a relationship with his own father.

I am reminded of Reva Devereaux's character from the

1991 movie, *Boyz 'n the Hood*. As a single mother, Reva was frightened about the future of her child, Trey. His behavior had become aggressive, and at ten years old, Trey was already known as the bully among his peers. Yet he was intelligent, and his mother and his teachers all recognized that. Reva realized that Trey needed his father, Furious, to be more involved in his life. She understood that she alone could only take her son so far.

So, as heart-wrenching as it was for her, Reva made the selfless act of a mother and put her son's needs for his father above her own. She decided to send Trey to live with Furious. As she dropped off her son, Reva made him look at her and she said, "I just don't want to see you dead or in jail." Then, Reva told Furious, "I can't teach him how to be a man...It's your job." Her point was clear: mothers can't teach a boy how to become a man. It takes a man to develop his son into a man.

The moment Reva pulled off in her car, Furious handed Trey a rake and ordered him to clear the leaves out of the yard. Respectfully, Trey obeyed.

I remember watching this movie, captivated by the growing relationship between Trey and Furious. One of the most memorable scenes for me was the scene where the two of them are on the shoreline having a father-son conversation while enjoying the ocean together. Seagulls looking for their meal soar across the waters and Trey boyishly hurls rocks into the ocean. This part was very interesting to me because this was the time Furious chose to ask Trey to recite the "3 Rules."

Trey recites: "Always look a person in the eyes. By doing that people will have more respect for you. Never be afraid to ask my dad for anything. And never respect anybody that doesn't respect you."

Cool, calm and collected, Furious butts in and tells Trey to break down those "3 Rules." He then adds, "Think before you answer."

What a great statement: *Think before you answer.*

I remember hearing the love behind that statement. Furious had purposefully downloaded virtues in his son that would be of great value to him. Furious understood the importance of thinking before speaking. He was giving Trey a life lesson on how not to react on pure impulse alone. At the age of ten, Trey received lessons from his father that many may never learn. I had to learn that lesson on my own, exclusively by trial and error. Furious also was teaching Trey to listen because he knew that good listening skills were crucial in learning to be productive.

Whether you agree with the "3 Rules" or not, you have to respect the father's position. He gave his son three simple things that he believed should be used in every facet of his life. I was very impressed by these two characters, especially because Furious was more than committed to the success of his son.

While growing up without my father, I had to find ways to develop my character on my own. What kind of lesson would my father have shared with me if he had been there, I often wondered? Would he have taught me things like the "3 Rules"? Furious taught his son to have integrity and to stand up for what he believed in. What did my father believe in?

What was my father good at? What did he have a passion for? Was he comical? Could he play a musical instrument? Could he play chess?

Back in elementary school I fell in love with chess, even though playing chess wasn't a popular game among all of my peers. But Lakeif Graves, Larry Combs, Todd Clark and I started playing chess when we were in the fourth grade. Being ultra-competitive with each other, we'd take advantage of indoor recesses and play. I'd win some and I'd lose some, but all in all I maintained a respectable record.

I remember when we started playing chess. We didn't have knowledge of the basics at all. Before we were able to start a game, we had to learn how not only to set the pieces in their proper spaces, but we also had to learn the role of each piece. From that we began to grasp the concept of the game. I must also state that there are many steps to becoming a chess player, in addition to the level of focus it takes.

After school and on weekends, we'd quickly roll out this old, dingy, black and white carpet chessboard measuring two feet by three feet. We'd place the large plastic black and white chess pieces in their appropriate spots. When we ran out of time and couldn't complete a game, we'd keep the pieces in position so that the game could be carried during our next break. We taught each other new strategies and techniques as our game improved. But before we gave any of our secrets to each other, we'd perfect them all first. I remember wishing I could go home and get some moves from my dad to take back to the table and use in my game.

As I've become older and as I've spent more time on the game of chess, I began to see the similarities between chess and life. In chess I had to pay attention to each move I made. Each move has to be made with intention. Moves made at the beginning of the game will determine the path I have to take, and those same moves can determine the outcome of the game. How I treat each piece is important.

All of the chess pieces are important, from the pawns to the king. In my younger chess-playing years, I used to think pawns were dispensable. That changed one day when another player put me in checkmate using a pawn and the queen. Then it hit me: each piece was equally important. Even though the pawn didn't have the capacity to move like the others, the pawn was the only piece that could rescue a piece that had been captured.

Likewise, I realized that each relationship in our lives is equally important. We should never underestimate the relationships in our lives that don't "move like the others," because one day we may need those relationships to rescue us.

In a similar way, the absent father has overlooked the importance of the relationship with his own child. That father does not realize that one day the "small people" in his life will become something significant and have the capability to rescue him. That father does not realize that each piece of a family is equally important.

We were never what I considered a "traditional" family. Having bedtime stories read to me was out of the question. Receiving hugs and kisses before bed or saying our nightly prayers wasn't even a thought. But I was very blessed because I had a strong mother. She knew one day that everything was going to be all right and that I would become a great man.

I seldom wonder if my father ever cared to know how I sounded, how I looked or how I walked. Did he care about my academic progress? Did I remind him of himself in any way? Did he ever care?

Even if God answered all my questions, it wouldn't change the fact that a man decided to leave an innocent child to figure out life on his own. Trial and error coupled with the help of others seemed to be the way I'd learn. I embraced being a doer and a risk taker, and I realized that life lessons can come from anywhere. So I learned to think by playing chess, and I got advice from Furious Styles, Cliff Huxtable and Chris Gardner.

If you could ask the father you never knew one question, what would that be?

THE SILENT CRY

My mother was very beautiful.

She stood five feet six inches tall. Her shape was like a sunset over the mountains, curves and light in personified perfection. Her beauty was both unnatural and breathtaking–a nightmare in motion, yet poetry personified–and none could tear their eyes away from her. It wasn't prettiness; it was much more than that. She had a real grace that was breathtaking. Her beautifully dimpled smile was infectious. Her flawless caramel skin seemed to almost glow in the warm sun, and her eyes were like pools of darkness.

To look into those eyes was to teeter on the brink of an abyss. When she fixed that gaze upon her prey, they knew they were in danger of falling. It used to make me mad when I would see guys in the grocery store vying for my mother's attention any time she was near. She could have been so much more–if only she had been whole.

After she died, I learned from my mother's journal that she had a hidden story inside her. Of course I read some things that I already knew, like the fact that she was only seventeen when she gave birth to me. But by then, she apparently had lived an entire life that I never knew about. Her journal testified that my father had molested my mother since she was twelve up until I was born.

Those perfect handwritten letters that were unmistakably hers on those pages hit me like a semi-truck running a red light. I was already hurting and that truth added to the sorrow. My mother never told me anything about being molested or raped. All my life I thought maybe my parents just didn't get along and they had decided to go their separate ways.

All at once, I understood. It made sense, why for years my mother never spoke about my father. It made sense why I never saw any pictures of the two of them together.

I sat there, holding her journal in my hands for a long time. In those moments, as I replayed my own past with my mother, I felt like I was watching a movie for the second time–catching details that I missed the first time simply because I didn't yet know how the story ended. My mind even tried to feed me horribly terrifying images of my mother as a child victim, but I tried my best to block them.

That man stripped her of one of the most precious and sacred gifts a female has: her virginity. As my mother gasped for air and cried out, no one was there to save her from that vicious lunatic. Only when he climaxed was my mother able to spell relief for a short period of time until he would attack again!

The exchanges between my mother and her abuser certainly were kept secret. She had to have been manipulated. I don't even know how that horrible man was connected to my mother in the first place. How did he have the level of access to her that he had? Were they next door neighbors? Where did he come from? How did he camouflage his efforts? Did anyone suspect him to be that kind of person? Was he an upstanding citizen? Was he trustworthy around his peers? Was he a menace to society?

I never knew my father personally. Several people have shared stories with me, however, and they will remain anonymous because this book is not designed to put my father on blast. This book is designed to raise awareness of fatherlessness in society across classes, races and ethnic groups. People said my father was a leader and he knew a lot of people. He was able to navigate through the streets pretty well. Others intentionally stayed away from him. Some said he was self-centered and arrogant. Regardless of the type of person he was or wasn't, he scarred my mother for life. And in my life, he was absent. After learning the truth, I wasn't sure if I ever wanted a relationship with my father, even if I had the opportunity.

My quest to find him meant nothing. He was heartless.

People say that everything happens for a reason, but obviously, my birth wasn't planned at all. On the other hand, if my father wouldn't have molested and raped my mother over and over, I probably wouldn't be here. Still, it's safe to say that no one was looking forward to my existence.

The new mystery for me then became to consider what my mother really dealt with physically, emotionally and mentally. There was no telling what she went through day after day, year after year. How did she manage to go through all of those years of abuse? How did she manage to shut off her pain long enough to be productive?

I can't fathom the things that go through the mind of a child who wants to fight and resist but feels so helpless. I couldn't imagine what it was like for my mother's cries to go unanswered, silenced by the distance between the violator and the people who could have helped. I wondered why she didn't tell her parents or at least another family member. Why didn't she tell a close friend? What did my father say or do to her all those years to keep her quiet? Maybe my mother did try to tell someone, but nobody listened. After all, she was just a little girl trying to voice her reasoning in a world full of busy grown-ups. I wonder if anyone ever asked my mother if she was all right. And I wonder if she pretended like everything was okay. She may have been able to fool others, but inside the depth of her soul she was wounded from top to bottom.

It is highly likely that my mother suffered from major grief, according to Dr. Laura Berman's website, "Grieving Stages a Rape Victim Goes Through." Trauma can cause lifelong scars that completely shift a person's paradigm. Dr. Berman also states that there is no prescribed way a rape victim should feel, and there are no specific benchmarks for overcoming the feelings that can arise after the abuse of a sexual assault. She concludes that the process of healing differs from person to person.

Whenever I look into the eyes of someone who has been sexually abused, I see it: the pain. I saw it some years ago when I had the opportunity to meet an eleven-year-old girl who had been impregnated by her father. She was eleven! When I saw her for the first and last time I thought she was in her mid-to-late teens. When I was told her age, I couldn't believe it.

I wanted to weep for the young mother as I watched her and her baby interact and enjoy the same cartoons that other children her age enjoyed. She played with her child more like a sister than a mother. Tears rolled down my face as I felt the loss she didn't yet know: she would miss her childhood completely in order to raise her child–her father's child. I thought about my own children, and just for a moment, I imagined that the girl was my daughter. I knew she would have to take care of her child while she was still being raised herself. And as her child grew, he would most likely begin to resemble his father. How confusing it would be for that young mother to love a child unconditionally who also happens to look like her abuser.

I wonder if my mother thought the same thing about me?

My mother never spoke about her childhood, and she certainly never mentioned any good times. She didn't share much about her past experience with her mother, father and her siblings. She kept her past locked up in a vault that even the strongest and best crew couldn't crack open.

My mother didn't have a lot of friends, either, though it seemed like she knew somebody everywhere we went. I imagine that people had let her down because she seldom trusted anyone. Maybe she felt like nobody would listen to her or maybe she thought what she said wasn't valid.

At the same time, my mother was stubborn. As frustrating as it was, when she made up her mind to do anything, she would not let anyone stop or change her mind. I remember her getting into heated arguments with my aunts or whoever else was there at that moment. Whenever I heard my mother yell, "Mikey, get the kids!" I knew it was time to go. We could be five miles away visiting my Aunt Phyllis (Aunt Phil for short), and if my mother was mad she even rejected Aunt Phil's offers for a ride home. Since we didn't have our own transportation, my mother would walk down Cleveland Avenue in the dark with us five kids. It was such a tiring walk, too. I remember in those moments, wishing we could have stayed at Aunt Phil's to finish playing. Most of the time, we would get about halfway home before my mother hitched a ride with someone she knew passing by.

Once we made it home, we went straight to bed and my mother wouldn't let us visit Aunt Phil's house for a while. She acted the same way no matter who argued with her. My mother had to have some serious grief issues for her to act like that.

On the other hand, Aunt Phil (whose real name was Phyllis Anne Butler) was a woman of wisdom and she had a strong compassionate heart for others. Aunt Phil always had plenty of food for everyone. She had nice furniture and the walls were filled with pictures of family. It felt like our own family art museum. I can remember on multiple occasions when there was a family get together, everyone went to Aunt Phil's. Back in those days, 1316 Republic Avenue was the place to be.

Family visits at Aunt Phil's were refreshing since most of us had to go home to a place that really wasn't the type of place we wanted to call "home." Going to her house gave us the opportunity to see what a real home was. Plus, she lived in a kid-friendly middle-class neighborhood. We always had something to do. We played games like hide-n-seek with the many kids who would flock to Aunt Phil's house. If we wanted to go somewhere, we played football or basketball at Linden Park with other kids from the community. Aunt Phil's home was not just the focal point for our family, but for the friends and associates of her children as well.

As part of our normal dialogue and childhood bonding, all the kids would gather up and play the dozens with each other. The dozens is a game of words between two individuals where participants insult each other until one gives up. This usually ended with someone being very offended, and sometimes, the arguments led to fights. It could be extremely cruel. At the same time, when we all got together and started to clown each other we were funnier than any comedian I ever heard. I still find myself laughing at some of the zingers that went flying between us.

Whenever we spent the weekend at Aunt Phil's, we knew that going to church on Sunday was mandatory. She had no problem making us sing in the choir either, which to me was really more of a male chorus. Aunt Phil was married to the late Reverend Clyde E. Butler (Uncle Butler). He pastored the New Canon Baptist Church located in a storefront building on the corner of Main Street and Champion Avenue.

Aunt Phil also had four biological sons: LJ, Shawn, Gary and Shannon. She also had two stepchildren: Clyde and Mary. From my perspective, everyone was treated with love and respect. Clyde was one of the coolest guys I ever knew. LJ and Shannon were the choir's lead singers. Shannon and I were the same age, and during that time, I was always moved by his boldness. Shannon led songs with so much passion and energy. He did whatever he had to do to captivate the audience with his stage presence. LJ could flat-out sing, and it was obvious he had a special anointing on him. To me, LJ was very mature. Not only could he belt out a tune, but he was a very good basketball player, too. LJ and Clyde also seemed to be the only ones who could put Gary in check whenever he'd pick on us. Gary and Shannon were two of my favorite cousins and we were all in the same age group.

I was never a singer, and in fact I hated having to sing, but if singing was going to get me over to Aunt Phil's then I was all in. To tell the truth, I hardly ever actually sang. I would lip-sync like "Milli Vanilli," hoping Aunt Phil wouldn't catch me and make me sing out loud.

We'd watch Uncle Butler sing his sermons like the Baptist preachers used to do. That was always humorous to me. My siblings and I would go home and mimic the church service. My sister Fee pretended to be the usher and Marv pretended to be the drummer. I was Uncle Butler or Uncle Ronald.

Uncle Ronald was my grandmother's youngest brother. Uncle Ronald had a real lively church when I was young. I didn't quite understand what he was doing, climbing over the pews while he was preaching. It was very entertaining to say the least.

Uncle Butler stood about 5'10" tall and carried a deep voice. I remember he was cool back then, so that meant he had a Jheri curl. He even nicknamed me "Hikey." Uncle Butler played a big role in the life of his children. They all had love and respect for him. He'd take them on fishing trips or to the beach, and he really seemed to enjoy family time with his kids. They'd travel together and take family road trips.

By trade Uncle Butler was a journeyman truck driver, and he spent a lot of time on the road. When it was time to discipline his children, he showed no mercy. His weapon of choice was a very thick, custom-made leather belt, and he could sling that belt off his waist like he was in a sword fight. But he never took his belt off unless he planned to use it. I would say the only downfall with Uncle Butler was that he had to spend a lot of time on the road, which meant that he was away from his children a lot, too.

There was only one problem with going over to Aunt Phil's house, and that problem was "Rusty," the meanest dog on earth. Rusty had the fiercest growl and he was always ready to attack. We were in straight fear while Gary and Shannon would fall out laughing at how frightened we were over their poodle. Yes, their fierce dog was a traditional, all-white, neatly-groomed poodle, and a crazy one at that.

I didn't have a pet, but I was four years old when my brother lil' Marv was born. Big Marvin (or Big Marv as I liked to call him) and my mother entered into a relationship when I was about one or two years old. I remember being happy to finally have a little brother to play with and to protect. At the beginning, lil' Marv's father was there for him. He took him everywhere he went. That was his boy–his first-born–and all of his family and friends knew he was his son. On birthdays and holidays, lil' Marv's father made sure he was there to celebrate. He always told him how much he loved him. Even after he and my mother split up, he made sure he spent time with lil' Marv.

I really didn't care for Big Marv, though. Even though he showed up for his son, he wasn't committed to having a family. He just came and went as he pleased. I could see the effect it had on my mother, not to mention my brother. If my mother ever got the feeling that Marvin was about to leave her, she would try to stall him by starting arguments.

We kids, however, had to deal with the aftermath of their fights. Once he was able to escape my mother's claws, she would take it out on us. Each time he left, drugs and alcohol swept through our home like a tsunami. My mother's eight-track record player blasted 1580 WVKO's Blue Monday oldies, and her "friends" swarmed through our house like bumblebees. This pattern went on for years and each year things got worse.

Two years after Marvin was born, my mother gave birth to Felice Rose Dean, and we called her Fee. She was my mother's pride and joy. Everything Big Marv did for lil' Marv he also did for Fee, but he never did any of those things for me. He would bring them things and take them places, but he always left me out. Without him saying it, I knew enough to know I wasn't his child. He wasn't particularly mean to me, it was just understood between us that I didn't have his support.

I don't know if he knew how his lack of support affected me. I can't say he didn't care for me. Every now and then he would let me go with them to a cookout or something. His family gushed over his children, yet not once did Big Marv introduce me as his son. After a while, I chose just to stay home if he wanted me to go somewhere with him. It was useless for me to go along and run the risk of feeling like a stranger in my own family.

Big Marv fought with my mother often, but I wouldn't call him "abusive." By the time my mother had her second child, she started drinking more and using drugs. I was around five or six years old when my mother started really getting into drugs outside of marijuana. My mother was the youngest of six, and on top of everything else, we were the "poor family" out of all my mother's siblings. We were treated like the "poor family" too, and by that time my mother had been on welfare for several years. Drugs and alcohol quickly had become the head of our house. Though my mother would try to hide it more so in the beginning, I wasn't a fool. Common sense told me something was going on when certain people would come over. They would have a few drinks and then go into a room with the door shut for about fifteen or twenty minutes. When they opened the bathroom door, a strange-smelling cloud of smoke poured out. I knew enough to know that something happened in that room that made them feel relaxed, satisfied and relieved.

Everybody in my family knew about it. I could tell by what my cousins said when we played the dozens. Playing the dozens could be funny when we were clowning around, but it could also be embarrassing and painful. We said cruel things to each other, which often led to arguments or fights. Even though I held my head up and threw my best shots to get even, on the inside I was weeping. We were taught, "sticks and stones may break your bones but words will never hurt you." We were very ingenious and had plenty to make fun of, but my cousins always came up with something that hurt worse. They even went as far as boasting about having both parents in the house and having a father who would teach them how to fish or who would take them to the beach. They used their words to cut deep and the wounds hurt.

I didn't envy them, but I wished things were different at my house. My cousins always had food in their cabinets. Their clothes were clean and were never hand-me downs. Going over to their house was always an adventure. During that time they did a lot of family things together. Birthdays and holidays for them were big celebrations. I couldn't envy them, though; I was glad somebody in my family had that kind of life. Despite how we acted as kids playing the dozens, my cousins were raised to be well-mannered gentlemen. More importantly, they were taught how to respect themselves and others.

I looked at the lives of my cousins and would say to the Lord, "Why me? Where's my daddy?"

I admit, I wasn't sure about sharing such personal information in this book. After all, this book is about fatherlessness, not childhood trauma or sexual abuse. But then I began to think about what I went through as a fatherless child, and then I thought about that eleven-year-old mother and her child. That baby will most likely grow up without a father, as well. That's when the revelation came to me that there has to be a direct correlation between sexual abuse and absent fathers. In addition, I want to encourage anyone who has experienced sexual abuse to tell someone your secret and get help to work through your pain.

Maybe you don't feel like you can reach out to your parents with something like what my mother went through. I am sure there are many who are afraid of what could happen as a result of speaking up.

We were taught as children, "When grown folk talk, you better close your mouth." We were taught that it was rude for children to interrupt adults, and often we carry that "hush-mouth" silence through our secrets and well into adulthood. You must find the inner strength to tell your parents, guardian, school teacher or family member if you have experienced sexual abuse. You have to speak up. By not speaking up, you are allowing further victims and the cycle to repeat itself.

I made the choice to share my story so that you might have the courage to share yours. Let the healing begin.

HOME AWAY FROM HOME: GIVE ME A FATHER

"Surrogate fathers are the safety nets in the lives of children. Without them, the children they have helped to raise and mentor would have shattered to the ground. They would have stayed broken like Humpty Dumpty, perhaps taking a lifetime to put the pieces back together. Although he may not be the biological father, the surrogate father exhibits love that is unconditional. These men must be commended for stepping in, and in many cases, taking the place of the fathers."
~Mike Dean

I didn't have many men who I could truthfully say I trusted, and who gave love and care in return. But my mom's older brother, Uncle Shug, was the closest thing I had to a father figure in my life. Words cannot explain what Uncle

Shug means to me. He helped shape me into the man I have become today. Uncle Shug was not perfect, but he was very noble. He taught me morals and he developed my character.

Uncle Shug was a very fair man and he loved our family with the love of God. If you were wrong, Uncle Shug wasn't afraid to confront you. If you did something good, he appreciated and celebrated you. But he also knew how to show tough love. And even during the times of tough love, there was some type of life lesson to learn. I didn't understand all of the life lessons at the time, but they stuck with me as I grew.

When I was a little boy, Uncle Shug enlisted himself in the United States Marine Corps. He was stationed at Camp Lejeune in Jacksonville, NC and he would make his pilgrimage home to Ohio at least twice a year. Once I grew up, he explained how hard it was for him to move away. His eyes grew teary as he later told me the toughest decision he ever made was the decision to leave his nieces and nephews behind. He missed out on a lot because he had to do what he felt was best for his future. As I listened to him, I hung on his every word like it was the final closing seconds of the Super Bowl game.

Truthfully, I'm not sure how life would have been for him if he had stayed home. Maybe his influence would have held our family together through turbulent times of drug and alcohol abuse. Maybe he would have become a preacher like our Uncle Ronald. Maybe he would have started his own restaurant since he is a great cook, or maybe he would have gone to college and played basketball. What I do know, is that if he would have stayed, he would have taught us everything he knew. He would have come to our games, and he would have been the one to come to our schools when we acted out or if we received awards. He would have put pressure on our family to be more supportive of one another.

When Uncle Shug was home visiting, he would pick me up and take me with him to visit his friends and family. When it came to family, he made sure to visit everyone, but he always stayed with my grandmother–the late Rosemary Dean.

Grandma... Words cannot express my love for that woman. I tear up and my heart grows warm every time I think of her. She was nothing but good to me. She kept to herself and she didn't like a lot of attention. Grandma was happy sitting at home, watching episodes of *Matlock* and *Perry Mason*. She cooked just enough food for herself, and when she needed something from the store she would ask me to go to the store for her. In return, Grandma always gave me some change. I'd purchase candy, pop or some other beverage or snack. She knew what was going on at my house, but she kept her distance from any drama. She'd be there to support us when we were low on food or household products. In fact, my family lived right across the street from her high-rise apartment. When I needed some peace of mind, I went over to Grandma's.

Whenever I knew Uncle Shug was coming to town, it felt like Christmas. I got the inside scoop on his arrival, too, checking with my grandmother every other hour as he traveled. Once I knew he was close, I would stay at Grandma's so I would be the first to greet him. I would wait for him as he pulled up in the parking lot of my grandmother's place. Then, I helped him carry his military-issued duffle bags into the house, and I stuck around while he got situated. Once he caught up with Grandma for long enough he would ask me, "Nephew, do you want to go with me?"

"Yes!" I replied eagerly every time. Then he would give me a specific time to meet him by his car so he first could freshen up after his long drive.

Once Uncle Shug was finished freshening up, I would meet him at his car as promised. He then drove to my house so that he could visit my mother. I never told her any of this ahead of time, so when we pulled up in his '85 Monte Carlo, she got very excited. I enjoyed seeing that excitement in her. No matter what my mother was facing at the time, her day was brightened by his arrival. I remember how she ran and sometimes screamed, "My Shug!" I remember my brothers and sister running right behind her and jumping into his arms as he received them all with love.

Once he finished talking with my mother, he would say,

"Sandy, Mikey is coming with me." And she hardly ever had a problem with that. Even if I was on punishment, Uncle Shug's arrival vetoed anything else we had planned. After we left my mother's house, Uncle Shug would say, "Nephew, do you want some White Castles?"

"Yes sir," I would reply with a big smile.

I enjoyed my uncle's visits. At the time he was the most important male figure in my life. He noticed me. I knew he loved me. The attention he gave me was authentic and I could tell it wasn't something he felt obligated to do. While we were together we always had talks. We would travel to see family members I hadn't seen in a long time. That always made it interesting and fun for me. When I spent time with Uncle Shug, I was able to escape the ugly reality I faced while I was living in the projects. With him, I didn't worry about anything. I just knew that he was tougher than Rambo and Conan the Barbarian put together!

One summer, Uncle Shug took me and my oldest cousin, LJ, with him back to North Carolina and we had a ball! I was able to meet my cousins: Shawn, Dorian, Ernie and Wally. Uncle Shug's wife was Aunt Carla, and she and I had an instant bond. She embraced me immediately from the start, and welcomed me into her home. In many ways, she gave me that fantasy "TV show" life I had always wanted. We had so much fun, and she treated me like a son. Even into my adulthood, she treated me the same way. She showed me so much love and I loved her so much in return. I admit it, she spoiled me rotten.

The summer was coming to a close and I didn't want to leave. What made it even harder was that Uncle Shug and Aunt Carla wanted me to stay. So Uncle Shug asked my mother if he could keep me for the upcoming school year. She said "yes" and I leaped for joy! I wished Marvin and Fee would have been with me, too. I thought about them every day.

Uncle Shug had to know what my life was like at home. We had many talks and he asked some tough questions. I got the feeling that my answers gave him enough information to fill in the blanks about how life was for me and my family.

During that school year with Uncle Shug, I made straight A's and B's. Aunt Carla made breakfast every day. Before we went to school, she packed our lunches, just like on *The Brady Bunch*. This was the life my cousins were used to, but it was all new to me. And if I did something wrong, I got punished just like everyone else. If I wet my bed at night, I'd be scrubbing the mattress, coupled with advanced potty training after my homework was done.

We played sports like soccer and football and we rode bikes. Where I'm from, we never played soccer, but in North Carolina joining in a pickup game was normal. My cousins were excited to have me there, so they quickly introduced me to the entire neighborhood. My cousin Shawn was the oldest out of the bunch, and he made sure nothing ever happened to me. Living with them, I knew I was far from the type of trouble typical in the projects. We often went to the beach to swim in the ocean, which was an experience all in itself. But before we went outside to play, we all had chores assigned to us and nobody was allowed outside until all the chores were completed. Aunt Carla always made sure our clothes were clean, too. Having clean clothes on a daily basis was unheard of at my house. Uncle Shug and Aunt Carla made sure all of our needs were met, and on a few occasions, we had some wants. I was happy.

During Christmas season, the whole house was decorated and the entire neighborhood was in the Christmas spirit. It was unbelievable! I'd never witnessed anything like it. We baked cookies and made fruit baskets. The house had the aroma of gingerbread and fruit. Of course I didn't believe in Santa. First of all, I never got what I wanted, and there were no chimneys in the projects. Plus, Santa didn't drink powdered milk, which was a dead giveaway for me.

I can remember the anticipation I felt on Christmas Eve. I could not wait to see what I was going to get. My mother always did the best she could, and I looked forward to her effort every year. But there was something different about that Christmas at Uncle Shug's. The feeling was something I hadn't experienced before. It was all new for me. My cousins knew what to expect. They knew that they would receive gifts that would make them believe in Santa.

I lay on the top bunk bed, tossing, turning and then straight staring at the ceiling, unable to sleep. All I know is I must have fallen asleep because the next thing I heard was Aunt Carla and Uncle Shug yelling, "Wake up! It's Christmas!" We all bolted out of bed and rushed to the living room like it was the final lap of the Daytona 500! I saw the most toys I'd ever seen in my life. I mean, the toys were brand names: Tonka trucks, GI Joe and He-Man action figures, along with many other toys.

Christmas lights shined on the ornaments, and fresh fruit and gingerbread fragranced the house. *Wait a minute,* I thought. Something caught my eye—it was a red BMX Western Flyer.

"Whose bike is that?" I asked Uncle Shug.

"It's yours," he replied. I couldn't believe it. I can't even explain how happy I was. That was by far the best Christmas I ever experienced as a kid. I was able to experience the ideal television version of Christmas, full of joy. I was so grateful.

I actually first learned how to ride a bike when I got my new bike for Christmas. Uncle Shug and the guys helped to coach me through the process. This was a BMX Trickster bike, which didn't come with training wheels. Uncle Shug was very intentional, and he had to be thinking, *Mikey will be able to ride this bike in no time; getting training wheels for him would be senseless.* I was relentless, doing all I could to learn how to ride and stay steady. Meanwhile, the others were riding trails and doing pop-a-wheelies. Learning to ride my new bike soon became an everyday thing. The king of all bike trails (with ramps) was nearby. I loved to jump those ramps, but trust and believe most of my landings weren't safe. It was obvious that even though my bike was a trickster, I was not. I'd fallen many times, but then I'd get back up and try again until I was able to jump with consistency.

Before I knew it, the school year was out and I knew that my time with Uncle Shug would be over soon. But I didn't want to go home. I wanted to make my home there with them. At the end of that summer, Uncle Shug told me that I couldn't stay any longer because my mother wanted me to come home. I told him that I didn't want to go.

Leaving behind "my home away from home" was tough. I slowly packed my bags and gave my goodbyes. Aunt Carla couldn't stand to see me go, and I did all I could do to get Uncle Shug to persuade my mother to let me stay. It was so bad that my mother told Uncle Shug if he didn't bring me home, she was going to send the police to his house. He had no choice but to take me back. Even though most of my family lived in Columbus, I felt like the best place for me to grow up was in Jacksonville with Uncle Shug and his family. As I grew older, I began to appreciate that at least for a short amount of time I was able to live a "normal" life.

Living with Uncle Shug for that year gave me a solid

perspective that will last my entire life. I was able to observe a married couple interact and communicate during their ups and downs. Uncle Shug indirectly taught me how to treat women with love and respect, and also he exhibited his love, passion and commitment toward his children. Every chance I get, I make time to visit Uncle Shug and Aunt Carla.

I'm not sure how my life would have been altered if I was unable to live in NC with Uncle Shug and his family. So much of perspective is based on experience, and through that experience I saw what "normal" looked like. I watched him go to work ranking up from E-1 (Private) to E-9 (Master Gunnery Sergeant). He has since retired from the Marines, but fulfilling a career in any military branch takes focus, drive, passion, wisdom, discipline and charisma. Uncle Shug knew how to follow orders from his superiors and he also knew how to give orders to those who served under his leadership.

I wouldn't trade Uncle Shug for anyone, anywhere. And from the paperboy to the small business owner, everyone loves Uncle Shug. He always has had the ability to put a smile on a person's face without their permission. To me, he is the most interesting man in the world.

At times, I still tear up thinking about how much Uncle Shug and Aunt Carla really cared for me. They cared enough to include me in their home and take care of me. They loved me and took care of me as if I was one of their own. That alone means even more to me now that I am a husband and father myself. I understand the cost and the time that it takes to take in an additional child. They truly had to have love in their hearts to be that selfless.

THE JOURNEY AHEAD...

On the road at 5:00 a.m. sharp back to Columbus, Ohio, I was silenced by the ever-changing view outside my window. Plains changed into mountain ranges, miles of farm country changed into small towns, and gas stations changed into rest stops. We zoomed through the countryside, going from one lane back roads to the interstate. My memory of an ocean view changed into nothing but waves of semi-trucks and speed demons flowing across the highway. My thoughts were plagued by the fact that I had to go back to a place called home.

Don't get me wrong, I missed lil' Marv, Fee and my mother; I missed them with all of my heart. But I did not miss the life we had to live. I didn't miss the drugs and alcohol. I didn't miss the drug dealers, prostitutes and drug addicts who seemed to plague my house. I didn't miss the rats and roaches. I didn't miss living in poverty.

I knew I had to go home. Then I thought to myself, *I ought to be grateful for the fact that I was fortunate enough to escape my life for a year.* It was over so fast. Staying with

Uncle Shug for two summers was simply a pit stop for me. I wasn't prepared for the journey ahead, and God knew I had to get gassed up to be able to endure the things to come.

I have a question for you: are you prepared for your journey ahead?

When I really think and reflect on the past, I can't say that I was prepared. What I can say is this: I was "gassed up." Anytime a car is filled with gas, the driver is then positioned with hope. Without gas, the driver has no hope for a destination. But with a full tank, there is confidence in the drive. As long as there is gas in the tank, the driver has strength to expect a destination. A life without expectation is equivalent to a car without gas.

After almost ten hours on the road, we finally arrived at my house. It was the first time Uncle Shug ever stopped somewhere else before he stopped at Grandma's. We lived in a second-floor, one bedroom apartment that was about six hundred square feet. The building was wrapped in old, beat up, white aluminum siding. It had a graveled parking lot and scratched-up black paint covered the metal stairs.

"Mikey!" my mother and three excited kids yelled at the top of their lungs. They were all screaming from the top of the stairs and greeting me with hugs, kisses and laughter. I recognized lil' Marvin and Fee, but I didn't recognize the youngest. I asked who the younger boy was.

"Rodney," they said, grinning from ear to ear. I picked

him up and gave him a big hug. I could tell that Rodney was just learning how to walk as he fumbled his way to me.

As I looked at them I wondered what must have happened to them while I was gone. They seemed so relieved to see me. It was as if a weight was lifted off of them. I was well-aware that coming home was going to take some getting used to. I was officially out of the pit stop and back in the race.

Later on that day, my family had a get-together over at Aunt Phil's house to welcome me back home. Gary, Shannon, Chris, Brian, Sherman and a host of other family members were in attendance. They couldn't wait for me to debrief them.

Then I noticed a guy in a wheelchair–my older cousin Shawn, plagued with cancer and completely blind. Within that small amount of time during my stay with Uncle Shug, things really had changed.

We were all happy to see each other again. I was telling them everything that happened while I lived with Uncle Shug. I didn't realize how much I missed everyone. They all made me feel right at home by playing the dozens. Everyone seemed to be in agreement that I had gained a significant amount of weight, which they found quite amusing. I must admit I packed on a few pounds, eating three full meals a day. They had fun teasing me about it, too.

Then my cousin Gary called me from the bottom of the

staircase. He yelled again for me, "Mikey, your dad is here!"

"What?!" I said as I shook with excitement.

"Your dad is here!" Gary said again.

Oh… I was super excited! My dad, my real dad! I was seven years old at the time, so I still had hope in my heart of meeting him one day. Boy, oh boy, this was it! Coming home after a year of being away and meeting my real dad all in one day! I dashed through the room and ran down the stairs. There, I saw a man standing with his arms out.

"Dad!" I yelled.

I jumped into his arms only to realize that it was Big Marvin. He gave me a big hug, and while I was looking over his shoulder I saw Gary laughing behind him. I didn't think it was funny. I had never met my dad and at that age it was my only dream. He knew who his dad was, and my hopes were maxed-out at the thought that I would know my dad, too.

My entire day was ruined by that joke. I'm positive Gary had no idea how much that would impact me. I started crying–hard. I cried because Marvin wasn't my dad and I wanted my own dad. Everybody had their dad–LJ, Shawn and Gary knew their dad and they looked just like him. Clyde, Mary and Shannon knew their dad. Tosha knew her dad, Sherman knew his dad, and Chris and Brian knew their dad. Lil' Marv, Fee and even Rodney, not only knew their fathers, but they had a relationship with him, too. They received birthday and Christmas gifts from their dads. But for me... It wasn't my reality. Maybe that's why Uncle Shug took me under his wing.

I learned six keys from my experience with Uncle Shug:

1. KNOW WHO I AM

I think this is what I loved the most about Uncle Shug. He showed me how to be a man and taught me not to be intimidated by anybody. He told me to always keep my head up and to not be ashamed of who I am or where I came from. He showed me how to take care of myself and embrace who God created me to be.

2. BE COMMITTED TO FAMILY

In other words, I have to do what it takes to envision my family in a better place. I must have a vision and an action plan that enables the vision to come to fruition. I must lay a strong foundation and build off of the fundamentals of life. That means it will take hard work on a consistent level. This also requires forward thinking, and keeping my family in mind during my decision making. Paying attention to the little things will give me the ammunition to conquer the big things.

3. LEAD BY EXAMPLE

Anybody can say what they are going to do, but not everyone is a doer. I've heard people say what they are going to do to improve their lives, but they just never seem to get it done. Uncle Shug was the opposite. If he said he was going to whoop me, I knew I was going to get it.

He never made promises he couldn't keep. When he said he was going to be there, he was there–on time. He never wasted a moment on foolishness and limited thinking. And he always gave me the truth, even if the truth wasn't what I wanted to hear. Plus, if he didn't know something, he was willing to learn from someone else.

4. NEVER QUIT UNDER PRESSURE

Whether we like it or not, we are "ranked" by the amount of pressure we can handle. The CEO of a bank has a different kind of pressure than that of a bank teller. The level of responsibility is different. Their daily activities are not the same. Where we are in life is a direct reflection of what we can handle.

One of the reasons Uncle Shug made it from a Private to a Master Gunnery Sergeant was because he was able to perform under pressure. Sometimes life will put you in "pressure cooker" situations, but how you handle those situations will determine the outcome. Uncle Shug taught me to never give up, even in the face of extreme pressure.

5. LIFE IS NOT ALL ABOUT ME

Uncle Shug taught me to live life in such a way that the generation coming behind me can benefit from my experiences. Life is made up of a series of experiences, and within those experiences there are people who journey with you and share in those experiences. Respect that people are entitled to their own opinions. Have a listening ear because you never know what lessons you can learn along the way. Most of all, understand that your way of thinking is not the only way of thinking.

6. ENJOY MYSELF AND OTHERS

Uncle Shug is a master at building relationships–when he walks into a room, the entire atmosphere shifts. His presence carried so much weight that people would line up just to have a moment with him. People made sure that he wouldn't leave without spending some time with them.

He made sure to speak to everyone he could, no matter who it was. That taught me that I have the right to create my own environment. I have the right to enjoy others and myself also. Most importantly, I can choose my influences.

To a degree this lesson taught me that happiness can be induced; it is maintained by the company I choose and the mindset I carry. I've learned how to choose to be around people who chose to be around me. I've learned to limit my time with people who do not contribute to the happiness in my life. That doesn't mean I don't love or care for an individual, but it does mean that I refuse to willingly compromise my joy.

The six keys I referenced are not things that Uncle Shug wrote down and handed to me on a sheet of paper, and they are not meant to be memorized and recited back like Trey regurgitating the "3 Rules." These are life lessons I captured just through being close to Uncle Shug. Those experiences taught me some truths that will remain in my heart, and I want to be sure I pass those same truths on to the next generation. The older I get, the more relevant those six keys have become.

My time in North Carolina filled my tank. What experiences in your life filled your tank?

MISSING IN ACTION - TEST OF TIME

*"I cannot think of any need in childhood as strong
as the need for a father's protection."*
~Sigmund Freud

The bell rang, school was dismissed, and the sound of elementary school kids yelling and screaming filled the air. A stream of yellow buses marked with black letters that read "Columbus Public Schools" flowed through the street. I always took a window seat because I enjoyed the scenery. I remember hoping the bus would have some type of malfunction, flat tire or engine problem—anything to cause a delay and let me enjoy the ride a little longer. Sometimes, I wished that the bus would circle the outskirts of the city simply because going home was something that wasn't always good. The air brakes squeaked until the bus came to a complete stop. When the door opened, I grabbed my book bag and walked down the narrow aisle.

We lived about two blocks away from the bus stop, and I took my usual route through the alley, which took me to the rear of our home. Along the way, I kicked a pop can. Only a few houses away and I would be home. I wasn't paying much attention to anything other than my next kick. Then, I looked up. Firefighters and squad cars crowded around my house. I burst into high gear, running with all of my might.

My house was burnt to a crisp; twisted siding the color of charcoal, deformed and smelted by the heat, was scattered around the charred front yard. The atmosphere was thick and it was hard for me to breathe. I panicked and my eyes swelled with tears. People were everywhere. I saw media covering the story, live. Investigators were questioning neighbors. An ambulance was onsite. I was petrified. *Where was my family? Did they make it?* I looked all around, but there was no sign of them. The more I searched, the more scared I became. Then, I thought I heard somebody calling out to me:

"Mikey…"

I looked around, but all I saw were the medics, the flashing lights and the smoke. Then, I heard it again:

"Mikey…"

"Mom… Mom… Mommy…?"

"Over here! Look behind you!"

I turned around and I saw them, my family wrapped in

sheets, sitting in the back of the ambulance. My mom was rocking back and forth. My heart was overjoyed with relief. My family was alive.

Apparently, my baby sister Fee had been playing with matches, trying to light a cigarette. My mom was asleep until she smelled smoke. She was able to get them all out, but they barely made it to safety. After the smoke cleared and the media and emergency response team left the scene, we looked around and realized that all we had left was each other.

We gathered everything we could salvage, and from there we began a journey I'll never forget. Already plagued by poverty, my mom was in no position to drum up the cash to stay in a hotel for the night or to find something long-term. We had no food and no transportation, but we put our trust in our mom. Even in tough times, she always figured out ways to make sure we had exactly what we needed.

Mom didn't waste any time. We began walking down the street carrying all of our belongings in wrinkled grocery and trash bags. It was quite a juggling act, constantly adjusting with unexpected rips and tears in the bags, and switching the load from side to side so it wouldn't seem so heavy or awkward. Silently within our minds we knew we were about to go into survival mode. What would be next for us? Where would we go from there? Where was my dad?

STORM AFTER THE FIRE

My mom reached out to her sister Aunt Loretta for help until she was able secure a place for us to stay. Aunt Loretta lived in one of the worst communities in our town called "Sullivant Gardens" (also known as "The Gardens"). She wasn't the type of person who did a lot of moving, either. In fact, she lived in the same community for many years–most of those years in the same apartment.

Even though she lived in a rough, poverty-stricken area, Aunt Loretta did her best to make room for us in her three-bedroom apartment. She had two sons living with her at the time, but we were all welcomed in with open arms. Staying at their home gave us some time to connect with each other, too. Plus, we were already familiar with their neighborhood since we had spent many weekends over there already. My big brother Nard was highly respected and he lived out there, too. For the most part, I was embraced by his peers.

The Gardens was one of those areas where you had to fight your way through, literally. Nobody was exempt from altercation. The people there lived by several rules, one being "never back down from a fight." Even if the results weren't in your favor, you never backed down. If you did, you quickly became labeled and then you were not immune to anyone picking on you. It was in your best interest to at least throw a punch and maintain your dignity.

My mom enrolled me into Sullivant Elementary School, but just when we were starting to settle in, my mother made us pack our bags and we were on the road again. She had a low tolerance for any opposition. So when I heard her and Aunt Loretta having a disagreement, and then I heard my mother's familiar yell, "Mikey, let's go," I knew all too well that it was time to gather my siblings and pack our bags. When she yelled "let's go," it meant we left right then. Weather conditions didn't matter, either. Rain, sleet or snow–when she said "let's go," we went. My mom never had a plan of action, either. We just went with the flow. And we kids never dared to question our mother. If we even looked like we were going to say something, we were liable to get popped in the mouth.

Aunt Loretta saw the saddened look on our faces as we slowly walked out the door. She tried to convince my mom to let us stay there until she could find some place for us to stay. Aunt Loretta never wanted their conflict to interfere with our safety, but we left anyway.

MOVING THROUGH THE RUBBISH

Those were rough, arduous and tumultuous years for me. We lived in some of the worst conditions. We managed to live on every side of town. Joyous moments were few and far between. Somehow, though, we coped with the life that we had to live. Tattooed by the trials of life, we cashed in hurt and turmoil like a man redeeming his chips in Las Vegas. The payoff, however, was hardly rewarding.

After short stays with family, friends and shelters, my mom finally found a place on the corner of Wilson Avenue and Forest Street on the south side of town. It was stationed on a corner lot that had four unit apartments with three bedrooms in each unit. The apartment was filthy when we moved in, and roaches had already staked their claim. It smelled like it had been vacant for ten years. Nothing worked properly and lead paint chipped around windows and door frames. The water pressure was too low to wash dishes, let alone take baths. The cold hardwood floors needed major repairs, and we learned very quickly that running through the house without shoes would guarantee a splinter. Nailheads poked out of the floor in some areas. The ceiling seemed to leak in every room when it rained, and dusty plaster chips fell on us when we moved through the place. By default, roaches seemed to be stationed in every place we lived. But we needed shelter. We had to adjust to our conditions because our conditions weren't going to adjust to us.

It was horrible.

But anything was better than being homeless. One time, we had to stay at the Salvation Army and there were only two twin beds for all of us to share. I could only imagine what went on in my mother's mind. Each day for her was a fight. I know she had many sleepless nights missing meals just to make sure we ate. I remember hearing her go off by herself to cry after she thought we were sound asleep. I could tell she was trying hard to weep in silence, so as not to wake us. Periodically I'd do my best to comfort her with a hug. Most of the time it seemed to work, and other times she just wanted to be by herself.

With all of our moving around that year, I ended up going to about six schools and I failed the fourth grade due to poor attendance. Moving from place to place never gave us a chance to establish ourselves anywhere. We'd make new friends, but by the time we got used to them we were saying goodbye. In fact, we learned to say our goodbyes in advance. We seemed to develop a knack for being connected and disconnected at the same time. Our situation groomed us to treat relationships much like people treat seasonal jobs.

Meanwhile, my mother did her best to replace the furniture we lost in the fire. We slept on the floor at first, which had become normal for us during that year. Then, people started giving us things. Soon, my mom furnished our home through the sheer giving of others. One day she walked in with mattresses for us so we didn't have to sleep on the floor. At times when we didn't have any food she'd come home with several boxes of food from the local food pantry. If she knew that the food pantry was going to give more than she could carry, I had to miss school to help her. Another day she'd come in and grab lil' Marv and me to help her carry a raggedy old couch someone didn't want any more. My mother fought hard to provide everything: a black and white television, a toaster, pillows, curtains and bed frames. We learned to treat used things as if they were new.

It was then that I overheard one of our neighbors tell my mother to keep our door shut because he saw a pregnant alley rat that was looking for a place to nest. I remember it was dead in the middle of winter, and our furnace wasn't working. Our best source of heat was for everyone to pile up in one room with a beat-up space heater. We pressed a couple of cloths up against the bottom of the door and did our best to preserve as much heat as we could. We even used my mother's prescribed heating pads to help us stay warm.

Despite our best efforts, that pregnant rat somehow crept into our old molded basement, and before we knew it, our home had been taken over by giant alley rats. The rats were barbaric and they were so big, they easily could have contended with a cat or a dog. We could hear them making noises in the basement day and night. Sometimes, it seemed like they were talking to each other. From then on, the basement was off-limits.

The rats would lay in the corners of our living room while we watched TV. I remember sitting in safety on top of the couch, and if I had to use the bathroom or make a move off the couch, I had to take the broom. I learned to hold the broom from the opposite end in case the rats attacked. If the broom wasn't handy, we used whatever else we could get our hands on to use as a weapon. There were so many rats that I couldn't keep count. It was terrifying, but we had no other option. After about two weeks, we let the rats have the house, and we moved to the Arms.

THE ARMS

"Bolivar Arms" was a dull, brown, brick apartment complex with windows made of black metal. Everyone called it "The Arms." The place was broken up into five sections called *circles*, and each circle had thirty or more units. Each circle was separated by a field that was about sixty yards long and forty-five yards wide, and vehicles had one way in and one way out of each circle. The Arms was designed to accommodate large families averaging six or more people per household. Ninety percent of the units were two stories, and most apartments had four bedrooms. We made our home at 980 Caldwell Place, Apartment 3.

The Arms seemed promising. The walls were painted and everything worked properly. The apartment had a clean refrigerator and clean floors, and all the windows and doors opened properly. Plus the place was kid-friendly with playgrounds and grassy fields.

My mother gave me a look that said, "This is it." Little did we know that our new home, seemingly filled with promise, would multiply to the third power all the trouble we faced in the past. Shortly after we moved in, I looked out the window and saw a park colorfully outlined with a roller slide, swings, tunnel and monkeybars. I asked my mother if I could go. Mother, being in a good mood, responded with a "yes."

When I got to the park, some kids from the neighborhood stepped in front of me.

"This is our park! Go home!" they said. I wasn't intimidated at all because I was bigger than they were.

"I'm not going anywhere!" I told them. At that, one of the kids swung at me, but I dodged the punch and pushed him down.

He got up looking mean and vicious like a king cobra filled with venom. "I'm getting my big brother," he told me.

"Go get your big brother!" I told him as he ran off.

But my heart dropped when I saw him return with a posse of some of the biggest kids in the neighborhood. I thought it was over for me as D-Train and Big Ed approached and fingers pointed me out. D-Train and Big Ed questioned me hard and left me with a "don't mess with us" talk. Then they stamped it by shoving me to the ground.

"You leave our brother alone or next time we will beat you up," they said.

Fortunately, I got the memo loud and clear and walked

away knocking dust and pebbles off my clothes. I went to school the next day ready to start over. That was when I met one of my best friends to this day: Andre Bass, more commonly known as Dre. The two of us hung with a few others and soon we all became like brothers. We played ball, went swimming at Maryland Park, or played freeze tag or hide-n-go seek. We rode bikes through the streets and trails. We were acrobatic and flipped off of dumpsters using old mattresses as springboards. We even called ourselves the "Flip Masters," challenging other crews in our neighborhood.

One day I was leaving school with Andre and the crew and they decided to detour by the monkeybars and do a few demon drops before going home. To do a demon drop, you start by sitting on the top of a bar that's about five to six feet off the ground. Then you fall backward, keeping your legs hooked to the bar. Once the momentum of the drop is built up, you release your legs and flip around upright in the hope of landing on your feet on the ground.

When I first saw Andre and the others doing it, I thought it seemed a little dangerous. But they talked me, the new guy, into doing the demon drop. Everyone was watching, and soon even outside spectators joined in. I was the center of attention.

If I am going to do this, I need to land on my feet, I thought. I rehearsed their instructions over in my mind, feeling the pressure. There was an ever-building audience of kids crowding around to watch the new guy do a demon drop. I was nervous sitting on top of the bar. *I don't want to get hurt or dirty from a bad landing,* I thought. *I've got to do this right.*

The pressure made me even more nervous since I hardly ever backed down from a challenge. What I didn't know was that the crew was testing me to see if they would accept me–accept me into an already established group of friends with a code that they held true to form for years. I held my breath and let myself fall back on the bar. Before I knew it, I felt the ground under my feet. I did it! There were high fives all around from everyone in the crew celebrating me. The whole thing gave me a rush and we did demon drops over and over.

It wasn't long before I got my landing and timing down to a science. As I landed my last drop, I came face to face with a guy I never saw before. He told me I couldn't do any more drops because that was his bar.

"I don't see your name on it," I said. But he made further threats. I instantly became angry. I didn't know the guy and he didn't know what my life had been like. So I punched him in the nose. Instantly, his nose gushed blood and he ran home with his younger brother.

Andre said, "Let's run! He's going to get his big brother!" As we ran, we laughed hard. I think that day got me into the crew. Then they started letting me meet the others when we got home from school. That's when they began to show me the ropes in the community so that I could navigate through one of the worst neighborhoods Columbus had ever seen.

BAD TO WORSE

It was all about survival and we didn't know what to expect from day to day. By 1992, our home life in the Arms was totally unpredictable and unsafe. Drug abuse, alcoholism and violence were at their peak in our home. I slept with one eye closed and one eye open. Drug trafficking was at an all-time high, and it seemed our house was the nucleus. Everyone from the neighborhood drug dealer, to the Detroit Boys, and even the Jamaicans came to stake their claim in our home that year, just like the roaches and the rats had done in our home before.

The Detroit Boys were a group of drug dealers from Detroit, Michigan who migrated to Columbus to sell drugs. They stuck together for the most part and would hurt anyone who threatened their business. They tried their best to create a low profile in order to dodge unwanted contenders and law enforcement.

The Jamaicans were similar to the Detroit Boys in their stick-together mentality, but when they wanted to hurt somebody, they did. They were smart and they thought strategically, but they also were ruthless. They came with the sole purpose of taking over. I'm not sure how my mother got involved with the Detroit Boys, the Jamaicans or the local drug dealers. All I know is that they were giving my mother drugs in exchange for the use of our home for whatever they wanted. They had all their weapons on them while they cooked their drugs in our kitchen. They used everything we had–silverware, cups, bowls, pots and pans–to cook up drugs. They'd leave drug residue on everything, and they never cleaned up their mess. I remember cleaning our dishes with extra care, especially when they were around. This lifestyle created hatred in my heart for that type of living. I HATED IT!

It was heartless, careless, and most of all, embarrassing. It was typical to see violent fights break out right outside of our apartment, or to be in the same room with an all-out brawl in our home. They damaged our possessions, shattered glass and broke windows. Victims with revenge on their minds would be beaten senseless, drenched in blood. The violence never ended, and even when things seemed like they were over, I knew they weren't.

They stashed their guns in our closets: 9mms, .45s, 12-gauge Mossberg high-powered semi-automatic rifles, and endless rounds of ammunition. Crack cocaine residue was in every jar, cup, pot or pan they used to mix and cook their drugs. Our television and radio stayed out of tune because they used our antennas as crack pipes. Even Big Marv stayed away as things got uncontrollable.

A friend of my mother's saw how unsafe our home had become, and one night he came to my bedroom with a look of concern.

"You are going to need this," he told me. He pulled out a chrome .25mm handgun and gave it to me. I couldn't believe my life had gotten so bad that an outsider felt that I had to have a gun. But I had no choice. It was solely to protect myself and my family.

By then, most of my peers had been absorbed or yanked into the street life on some level. Some were in deeper than others. Most just wanted to keep money in their pocket, while others just wanted to look like they were drug dealers, but really they weren't. Some of them were trying to emulate *Scarface* and many achieved that goal in their own way. Those guys were teens or young adults and the drive was all about money. They would do anything to ensure they made it. The sad part is that most of the people I grew up with ended up in prison. Seeing them escorted off by the police was always a sad time. Most of their mothers or fathers were users, hustlers or were incarcerated, so they gravitated toward the street life by nature.

The saddest part about the street life is that many innocent bystanders lost their lives just by being in the wrong place at the wrong time. These were people who had nothing to do with that life, but who instantly became a target when they decided to party or chill with some friends from the street. Most times people who said they didn't want anything to do with street life were lying, anyway. They may not have wanted to rob, cheat or steal, but they enjoyed getting high and hanging out with the females, trying to score some sex. But when it comes to that life, people can't pick and choose. The street life was a controlled environment. Everywhere I went I saw it. Going to school and trying to pursue an education wasn't even on my mind. We were all just trying to survive and make it to the next day. In all actuality, going to school was a great opportunity for a short moment to escape the life we were living every day.

I could have attached myself to that life if I wanted to, but I didn't. I didn't want to sell, or even do drugs. At school, I had major anger issues and I got into fights on a weekly basis. The teachers liked me, but I often gave them problems. Needless to say, my first year at Centennial High School did not go well academically. I don't recall ever doing much homework. Doing homework or studying for anything was nearly impossible under the conditions I faced at home.

I went to school with just about everyone from my hood. Centennial was a mixed school, way out in the suburbs of Columbus. Caucasian students made up the majority of the student body at the time, and African Americans came in a close second, sprinkled with Asians and African foreigners. We had some of the best administrators and teachers, too. Even with all of our issues, the teachers really seemed to care. In spite of that, though, people dropped out of school in record numbers. They dropped out so that they could be full-time drug dealers. Some of them had to help with the bills because having a parent on drugs was not only embarrassing, but financially taxing at the same time. Drug addiction caused parents to spend bill money, sell food stamps and pawn anything that was worth something. A lot of parents put themselves in a bind by getting credit from a dealer in the middle of the month, which caused them to forgo at least twenty-five percent of their welfare check, if not all of it.

Needless to say, going to school with the weight of the world on my shoulders made it difficult to stay focused. Most mornings, I was already mentally and physically drained by the time I got to school. I saw some of the most talented people–gifted people–never fulfill their dreams, simply because of their circumstances. But which was more important: having a safe place to stay or making it to English class? Which was more important: eating that day or taking the ninth grade Proficiency Test?

I remember going to school in the frigid winter weather with no socks to wear. I remember going to school tired after being up all night listening to people arguing and fussing at one another. And, if I had taken any books home, chances were that a few roaches would try to hitch a ride back to school with me the next day. I remember hearing the other kids laugh when stowaway roaches crawled out of my shoes or books on days I forgot to shake out my things before school. It was funny to others but it was never funny to me.

Mom! Where Are You?

I remember my mother left us for a few days without any notice or adult supervision. Not knowing where my mommy was scared the life out of me. She stayed out for long periods of time before, but it was uncommon for her to stay away that long. I looked everywhere for her. I went to every friend and every hangout spot to find her. I tried my best not to panic or let my siblings see me panic. They'd ask me on several occasions, "Where is Mommy?" I kept telling them that she would be back.

I fixed dinner and made them get their clothes out. I put them to bed and then walked around the hood for a few hours searching for her, hoping that she wasn't lying dead in a dumpster.

"Have you seen my mom? If you see her, tell her I'm looking for her," I said to everyone I knew. It was my sales pitch. Finally, I had to get home to make sure my siblings were safe. After that, I waited up for her to return. I waited and waited until my eyes got so heavy that I fell asleep hoping she would come home by morning.

I woke up in the morning and looked around the house, but she still wasn't home. No school for me that day. I woke up the kids and sent them off to school, instead. Once they were safe, I'd continue my search. I was nervous, confused, and most of all concerned. I wasn't thinking about a math test or a science project. I wanted my mom to come home! No one knew where she was.

"Mikey, have you found Sandy?" asked Sissy Pie, one of my mom's friends.

"No," I replied. Sissy Pie was like an aunt to me, and she quickly grew concerned. She did all she could do on her end to support us and help find my mother without letting the entire neighborhood know about it. People would have called Children Services on us if they even got a whiff that we were abandoned.

We still couldn't find my mom, so the next day I did the same thing I did the day before. I even searched in a few more places that Aunt Sissy Pie suggested. You can't imagine some of the places I had to go into to try to find my mom. I was fearless and scared at the same time. But I was determined to find my mother by any means necessary.

Day two came to a close and still there was no sign of Mommy. My brothers and sister were little, but they weren't fools. They knew something was wrong. The youngest started whining, "I want Mommy!" over and over and over again, which started a chain reaction of emotion. Throughout this entire ordeal, my eyes got glossy and I tried not to break down myself. Between caring for my siblings and searching for my mom, I was exhausted-averaging two to four hours of sleep each night.

On the morning of the third day, I jumped up and routinely searched the house, hoping she had returned in the middle of the night. Sadly, she still wasn't home. I was running out of options. I knew I would have to miss another day of classes, but I refused to let my sister or brothers miss school. At school, they were guaranteed to eat two meals each day. School also gave them a safe place to be while I searched for our mom. It also gave me time to weep without anyone around.

It was the end of day three. The lights were out for the kids, and they were quickly sound asleep. Shortly after midnight, my mother stumbled in the house with a bloody mouth and a missing tooth. It looked like she had been in a fight. I was shocked.

"What happened?" I asked.

"I slipped on some ice," she said.

Of course I didn't believe her. But, I didn't ask any more questions. I just let her be. I was so happy that she was alive. Thank God she was alive!

I went back to school the next day, but I didn't tell any of my teachers what went on in our home that week. I simply kept a straight face and told them that I didn't feel like coming to school. I did my best to catch up with my missing school work, but by then I was too far behind.

MISSION POSSIBLE

Having a father in my home may not have prevented these situations, but at least we kids would have had a protector. The drug dealers may have still camped out at our home, but at least we would have had some line of defense. Having a father in our home would have been like border patrol on an international line–everyone would have to go through customs. But when the father is missing in action, there is no resistance for any type of invasion.

> "How in the world do you think it's possible in broad daylight to enter the house of an awake, able-bodied man and walk off with his possessions unless you tie him up first? Tie him up, though, and you can clean him out."
> ~Matthew 12:29

Fathers, wherever you are, you can escape your bondage. You are more than capable of being the best father you can possibly be. Fathers, you are born leaders. You may not ever become a CEO. You may not ever get your degree. But you are built by design to lead your family. Even though you may be missing in action, your ability to be the best father you can be is not an impossible mission.

CRACK: HEAD OF THE HOUSE

"It is easier for a father to have children than for children to have a real father."
~Pope John XXIII

Once crack cocaine busted in the homes of our community, it caused total chaos. It massacred the black and brown communities. It had no respect for any person and it literally ripped families apart. Crack affected everybody I knew. If parents weren't on it, their kids were secretly selling it. It got so bad that families were selling crack to each other without regard–sons sold it to their mothers or fathers. Daughters dated drug dealers, or else they sold it, or even used it themselves.

Crack controlled everything. It vetoed positive reinforcements and it desensitized us with pinpoint accuracy. Crack was being sold every day on every corner in my community. Many people lost their lives as a result of crack violence. I think it would be an understatement to say that in my community, crack was worshipped.

The streets were like *Night of the Living Dead*. Because dope fiends did anything to get it, relationships were torn apart. Husbands and sons filled up the prisons. Drug dealers started hustling early as pre-teens because it didn't cost as much to start early.

Established dealers gave new dealers drugs upfront, more than doubling their investment in a matter of hours.

Once the crack epidemic hit my community, even the dreams of the people changed. Before crack took over, our community had many model citizens, potential politicians and potential professional athletes. These same people, however, went from potential politician to gunslinger, and from potential professional athlete to high school dropout.

Often I wondered if the infestation of drugs was more about race or class. With the implementation of crack into the streets, drug cartels and local drug dealers weren't the only ones who benefited from the epidemic. At the time, the lower-class communities were growing steadily. Once drugs took over, more law enforcement had to be employed and more prisons had to be constructed. Law firms increased, bail bondsmen multiplied and endless laws were created, all to manage the influx of drugs in lower-class communities.

Hollywood glorified the street life by producing movies

including *Boyz 'n the Hood*, *Menace II Society*, *New Jack City* and *Blood In, Blood Out*. Guys ditched dreams of going to college or becoming a carpenter like their fathers or grandfathers. Instead, they aimed to be kingpins like Nino Brown, killers like O-Dog, and gangsters like Tupac Shakur. Even the music reflected the crack epidemic. Rap videos filled our minds like a cold glass of Kool-Aid in the heat of the summer. I watched crack change my community from being called a neighborhood to being called "the hood." Soon, there was nothing "neighborly" left.

The people who lived in the community used to own the businesses there, and they weren't trying to "get rich or die trying." They knew our families and they would tell our parents if we did something wrong. They even provided other families with credit in their stores because they knew when times were hard. People looked out for each other, but it wasn't long before most of the black-owned businesses had to close their doors. Foreigners embraced this cosmic shift and began to take over every store in the community. They marked up all of the prices and they sold cigarettes and alcohol to minors without a second thought. Soon, black-on-black crime became normal.

Crack affected absolutely everyone, and my family was not exempt. On top of my mother's relational issues, the epidemic crept in our home like a thief in the night. When my mother's "friends" migrated to our home, we kids learned how to keep ourselves as safe as possible. We knew to go outside if it was daytime and to go to bed if it was night-time. It got so bad that drug dealers would have sex with my mother's female friends in our bedrooms just to fuel their habit. My baby sister Fee's room was highly attractive for sexual activity because she kept it clean, neat and organized. I remember times when she would be sitting on the stairs at the age of six, waiting for a drug dealer and some of my mother's "friends" to finish. I hated seeing my sister sitting like that, balled up tight on the top of the stairs with tears streaming down her little face. She would wash her sheets by hand each time. We never had a washer that worked, and instead of a dryer we had to hang everything on doors, chairs, shelves or anything else that was vacant. Fee would re-clean and re-organize her room, and then she would complete her homework. What a sad and tragic upbringing for a six-year-old girl!

When Marv was there we didn't have to go through that, though. Every two or three months, he came to stay for a few weeks. And as much as I didn't like Marv, I knew that during that time we wouldn't have to worry about chaos. We actually had a little peace during those times, but once he left, the invasions started right back up again.

Even during all of our chaos, our mother tried her best to keep us healthy. She took advantage of the health care provided through welfare, and she paid enough attention to become concerned when she found a lump in her breast.

I was twelve years old when my mother walked in the house teary-eyed and told me that she had been diagnosed with breast cancer. She further stated that the doctors said she had less than nine months to live. I loved my mother so much that words can't even begin to express how much I loved her.

"You are not going to die," I told her. From that day forward I prayed every day that God would heal her. We couldn't possibly lose our mother. We were all we had. My mother taught us to stick together and she taught us to defend each other. For our mother to die at the age of twenty-nine would have crushed us. Family support probably would have been limited, and it would have been nearly impossible for us kids to grow up together. We were sure that if our mother was gone that we would have been split apart. We were all young; JD was three, Rodney was five, Fee was six, Marv was eight, and I was twelve. It would have been tough for anybody to take us in and provide the proper care for us. None of our family members would have let us go to the system, though. They would have done all they could to make sure we were raised to the best of their ability. But most of all, it would have devastated us to lose our mother.

I didn't know much about God or prayer, but I had heard people during the testimony service stand up and say that prayer changed their situation. I felt like I needed to give prayer a shot. I didn't know what else to do to keep my mother alive. I prayed for my mother every chance I had. I didn't let a day go by without saying a prayer for her. I also vowed to myself at that point that I would never lie to her, even if I would be punished as a result.

My mother survived breast cancer, despite losing a breast. Even though she had major personal struggles that prohibited her from having a productive life, to me she was amazing.

THE PARK

I knew my father had been watching me from a distance. I remember one early afternoon during the summer of 1988. I was about twelve or thirteen at the time. Tonya, one of my mother's friends, saw me and said, "Mikey, I just saw your dad. Just go around there and see him. He's at the park. I just saw him."

"Who? Marvin?"

"No. Bill. Go ahead. Go see your dad."

I instantly got excited. My dad! I dashed to the park, running at the speed of light. I couldn't believe that I was finally going to get to meet him!

But by the time I made it to the park, he was gone. I looked everywhere, but I didn't see him. I didn't see anybody there. Did Tonya really see him? I looked left, and I looked right, but the hopes of finally meeting him slipped through the crevices of my fingers like sand in an hourglass. There was no way he could have left the park before I made it there. It was only about twenty seconds from my house. So I began to walk around to see if I could spot someone who looked unfamiliar to my neighborhood. Surely, he couldn't have gone far.

At that point, my heart was still open enough to call him "Dad." I wanted to show him that I had good manners. I wanted to show him my jump shot, so he could critique it and give me pointers to help enhance my game. I was hoping he would take me with him when he would go somewhere. I wanted to ride in the front seat, wearing his sunglasses that were far too big for my adolescent face. He could tell me who I should trust and who I shouldn't trust. Perhaps he would encourage me to recite the three C's. He would stress the importance of earning an education and encourage me to not make the same mistakes he made in life. I was still open for all of that, but it never happened.

Mr. Jones

By the time I was in the ninth grade, I did my best at school, but Mr. Jones had it out for me. He was my history teacher. Mr. Jones wasn't a bad person, but he was set in his ways. When he had favorites, he made sure that everyone in the class knew who they were. I was a class clown by nature, and there were at least two other class clowns in each of my classes. The pressure to "perform" often took center stage, and Mr. Jones hated our behavior. Plus, he was ill-tempered, especially because he was nearing the end of his career.

I'll never forget when Mr. Jones threatened me and two other students. In front of the entire class, he said, "Michael, Markus and Jermaine, on the last day of school I'm going to kick your [butt]." He didn't use that exact language, though. Instead, he used a few choice words. None of us felt threatened by him, especially because the three of us guys were all on the football and wrestling teams that year. Still, Mr. Jones did threaten us. I think I was offended by his words more than anything.

Immediately following our class, we went to our school administrator and told him about the threat. He didn't believe us and sent us off to our next class. It was obvious that there wasn't going to be any investigation into this matter, and in the back of my mind I knew Mr. Jones was serious. His threat was made early in the school year. By the time finals week arrived, everyone was ready for the year to be over, including Mr. Jones. All his students had already finished taking his final exam earlier that week, so his actual class period was nothing more than free time.

With time to kill in the classroom, Mr. Jones spouted off on a rabbit trail about how the African American students should be more like the Asian students. He went on and on, contending that the African American students in the classroom didn't understand his point. He was right about that. Mr. Jones was African American himself. Frustrated, several of us raised our hands to ask him if we could be dismissed out into the hallway until the next period because it was apparent he wasn't going to stop putting us down. He let Markus and Jermaine go. Then Chrissy asked to go, too, and he let her. But he ignored my raised hand. I kept my hand up and even called out, "Mr. Jones," but he still ignored me. Finally, I said, "Forget it!" I then got out of my seat to go to his desk and ask him.

While I was walking toward him, he watched me. Before I could say one word, he said, "Don't touch me." Then he turned his back, trying to ignore me again. I tapped him on his shoulder.

All I remember after that was his old, raspy voice and the "husk, husk" sound of a two-piece punch coming to my face. My instinctive reaction was to spear him across the room through all of the desks and chairs. In a matter of one second, I had my knees on his arms so he couldn't hit me again, and I was proud of myself that I never punched him back. It wasn't worth it, and I knew he couldn't beat me anyway. I knew I was in trouble, though, but I didn't want him hitting me again. I was defending myself. While I restrained him in that position, he repeatedly yelled, "Get off of me!"

Suddenly, another teacher snatched me off of him and dragged me down the hall. I told him over and over what happened in the classroom, and my classmates soon brought credibility to my statements. The next step was to have my mother come in to the school to have a conference with school administrators and with Mr. Jones.

When I got home and told my mother what happened, she assumed I had done something wrong. I'd already had my fair share of run-ins at school between fights, insubordination and other disruptions. I tried to explain that the teacher attacked me first, and that I had a classroom full of witnesses to corroborate my story. I tried to tell her that we had a lawsuit on our hands, but she didn't listen. My mother didn't want to go all the way out to Centennial High School. It was a far ride, and she had to find a ride for us to go out there. She cussed me out the entire way there, even popping me upside my head a few times before the meeting started.

After the meeting, the administrators ended up doing an internal investigation. They found Mr. Jones guilty. The administrators then made a deal with my mother and broke down their terms. Since I didn't have the grades to pass school that year, they decided to pass me anyway with the agreement that I wouldn't return to their school. My mother took the deal, and I was hurt by that. I wanted to pursue a lawsuit and sue whomever we could sue. My mother just wanted the whole thing to be over. Mr. Jones was never fired.

I'm not sure if he was disciplined at all, and I was the one who had to suck it up and get ready to attend another school.

GAME CHANGER

That next night was different than any other night. It all started with Butchy wanting to go to the store. Butchy was like a little brother to my mom, and he was the one who gave me my first gun. The two of us actually had the same gun, but we had only one clip and one set of bullets to fill the clip. Butchy said he was going to leave the clip with me so I could protect the house when he went to the store. I felt like things were pretty secure at the house that night, so I told him that he would need the clip more than I would. We went back and forth a few times until I persuaded him to take the clip with him for his own safety. Walking around at night in my community brought unpredictable threats–real life and death threats–not just offensive words from people like Mr. Jones.

Butchy no longer refused my offer, so he took the clip. My mother never knew about our conversation, and she certainly never knew I had a gun. She was downstairs with a friend, talking. I lay back down in my bed, but I wasn't asleep. I was just laying there thinking about days being better and what it would be like to go from rags to riches.

Ten minutes after Butchy left, I heard someone knocking on the door. My mother asked her friend to get it.

"Who is it?" her friend asked through the door.

"It's Louise. Let me in," said the voice on the other side of the door.

My mother's friend started to unlock the door. What she didn't know was that Louise was being held there at gunpoint by a member of one of the most infamous gangs in the city. Once that door began to open, gang members forced their way into our house. They beat my mother's friend horribly. She was a very small lady, standing only about five feet tall and weighing around a hundred pounds. Soon she was knocked out and bleeding all over the floor. By then, I had made my way to the corner of the steps, wishing I would have listened to Butchy and kept the clip.

I knew who they were. They were the "Riders," and they were notorious. They terrorized everyone. The leader and the other main gang leaders lived in the same circle we did. I used to look up to them, too. We'd marvel at how the Riders would go to the trunks of their cars to grab guns and chase other cars down, emptying their clips all on one car. That's what happened whenever an unwelcome outsider came to the hood. Outsiders barely escaped the rapid gunfire. Things like that happened in broad daylight. The Riders were so bad that they would give a guy drugs to sell, and once he came up, they would rob him of all of his money and then put him back to work on the streets again. But even as horrible as the Riders were, I never expected them to terrorize us in our house the same way they did with everyone else.

From the top of the stairs, I could see their shadows and I knew I was too small to fight them. I would have gotten killed, for sure. Then I saw the leader put his gun to my mother's head.

"Tell your sister I want my money," he hissed at her. My mother was shaking and trembling while she bled from the hit she took from the back of his pistol. I knew she was scared for her life. She tried to persuade them to stop beating her frail friend who was already knocked out and bleeding profusely.

"I'll tell her," she said, crying.

"I should kill you, but I love your kids!" the man told her. Then the Riders all began raiding the place, taking anything and everything they could. I crept back to my room like a ninja, not knowing what was going to happen next.

Then, I jumped out of the two-story apartment and ran to my friend's house. I remember crying while his family let me call 911. My friend's name was Ryan, and his father and grandmother wouldn't let me leave until the police showed up, which took forty-five minutes. It was typical for the police to arrive way after an event was over, unless they wanted to satisfy their own interests. By the time they got to my house, the Riders were long gone.

Once the police left, I was left walking through a house full of broken glass. I looked at all of the damage to the house. I looked at the blood on the floor and the chaos in every room. Then, I looked at my mother.

"We have to move," I said.

CAN'T CALL YOU HOME NO MORE

DESTINATION NEXT

It was finally time to move. My mother and I were in full agreement on leaving behind what we once called home. At this point, I knew I was going to be leaving some of my closest friends, but it was too dangerous living there any longer. Being the victim of such a violent act was too much. What would happen if the Riders had a change of heart and wanted to do more harm to us? We were sitting ducks and safety and security were first priorities. The police certainly weren't planning on making any arrests. It was no longer a place we could call home.

My mother went out and found the first available place she could find. We packed our bags almost immediately. Anything was better than being in the targeted view of one of the most notorious gangs in Central Ohio.

I honestly thought things would get better since we made

the pilgrimage to an unfamiliar side of town. But things got worse. In fact, it seemed like we picked right back up where we left off. Drug and alcohol abuse didn't exactly abandon ship, either. It didn't even walk the plank, nor did it surrender to change for the better. During that time, there wasn't such a thing as "change for the better." The drug infestation never packed its bags. Plus, we moved out of CMHA housing (Columbus Metropolitan Housing Authority), which meant that we were once again under the jurisdiction of a slumlord. CMHA had maintenance that did repairs on the apartments as needed. But slumlords were just property owners who didn't address the real-time needs of the property or the tenant. So in our new place, nothing worked. The hot water tank, toilets, sink faucets, refrigerator, outlets, doors, and even the door knobs had problems. All of the appliances supplied by the landlord were old and outdated. In fact, we went that entire winter without a working refrigerator. I remember putting our perishable items in covered boxes outside so our food would stay fresh. Even so, living there was better than having to live in fear of the Riders coming back to our home.

Playing sports, primarily basketball, was my outlet, and I was on the court faithfully. I started out hardly knowing anybody, but as time progressed, I began to gain respect from other regulars on the court. People started to ask my name, where I was from, and where I would go to school in the fall. Every so often, I would run into someone from my past who would endorse me to the new guys, furthering my growth both in relationships and basketball.

My mother, however, attracted the same type of people that she had before. Again, drug and alcohol abuse staked its claim in our home. Some of my mother's longtime friends even followed us from our old place to our new one.

THE DIFFERENCE MAKER

I had some of my most memorable moments at my new school, Walnut Ridge (Ridge) High School. Ridge had mostly a middle-class population and it didn't have nearly as many poor blacks as Centennial did. Ridge also had a spirit of family support, which I loved. Many students lived in stable families and received support from their parents. I also noticed a difference between the kids who had family support and those who didn't.

Jawanza Moore, for example, had both of his parents at home and both of them worked. Jawanza was a 3.0 student athlete and was one of the best basketball players in Ridge history. His dad seemed to be at every game, too, cheering on his son. Jawanza tried to play even harder when he saw his dad in the stands.

"That's my boy!" his dad would yell at the top of his lungs. And I can only imagine the conversations the two of them had when they got in the car.

"Good job, boy," I imagined Mr. Moore told his son. Even when Jawanza had bad games, his dad encouraged him: "Son, you'll get them next time." Jawanza's dad even helped him with his jump shot, and he made sure to sign him up for any camp that would improve his game.

But when I looked down the bench, most of the team didn't have a dad like Mr. Moore. Even though the school in general had a spirit of family support, many of the other players never once saw their dads at a game yelling, "That's my boy!" We all wanted that, not just when we were on the court or in the classroom, but we wanted that kind of support to learn how to be a man, a father and a husband.

I wonder if Mr. Moore knew the impact he had on his son. I wonder if Mr. Moore's father had been there for him. Did he receive family support as a boy? Is that how he learned to give family support? I wonder what Mr. Moore learned from his own father that made him such a successful father himself?

By my junior year at Walnut Ridge High School, I had a positive attitude and my grades were good. I loved going to school. I liked all my teachers and they were all very respectful and caring toward me. I had made friends from the basketball team, the marching band, the chess club, the automotive crew, the wrestling team, the football team and the track team. I knew people everywhere, but my main focus was completing school and playing basketball. After that, I wanted to go off to college and play more basketball. I knew I had to do well that year if I wanted to have a chance to go to college. So I vowed to do whatever I needed to do to stay out of trouble and maintain good grades. I was a young man on a mission, and I had a lot to prove, especially on the basketball court.

During that summer I played against most of the major talent in the Nike basketball summer and fall leagues. Going to the NBA was on most ball players' minds, but my main concern was to have the opportunity to play during my senior year. I also really wanted to help lead my school to a city championship. My plan, however, wasn't as foolproof as I thought.

THE BOILING POINT

It was a cold, wintry night after dinner, and my mother threatened to kick me out of the house again. This wasn't the first time, and I didn't take her seriously. But at that point, I decided that if she ever again told me to get out, I was going to leave for sure. I would leave and never look back, no matter where life took me. I was tired of my mom threatening me over and over again. For the most part, I did everything I was told until I got so fed up with the life we were living.

I began to come home after curfew, just in time to go to bed. That's what made my mother so angry. I thought it was unfair to be punished for spending time with like-minded friends. As far as I was concerned, the punishment was worth it. My behavior was really just a way to have short pockets of escape from my reality. And the punishments were temporary anyway. I knew that as soon as my mom's friends came to the house, the drugs got me off punishment.

My mother was hard on me. I assumed it was because I was the oldest. Other than that, I saw no reason for her to be so tough on me. Even though my mother loved us with all of her heart, it was the drugs that took my mom away from us. After all we had already been through, crack was still the head of our home.

I watched drug dealers who thought they were macho after seeing a Mike Tyson fight. They'd play chicken with my mom's male friends, thinking it was fun to knock a defenseless man senseless. Blood gushed everywhere until the man was unrecognizable. Nobody dared fight them back, either, for fear of losing their lives. They just let the drug dealers toy with them. All I could do was watch, and it made me hate drugs and everything they stood for.

I remember one particular school night during that same winter, my mom ran into our room in total panic.

"Mikey! Dwight is killing Lonnie!" she screamed at the top of her lungs. Lonnie was paying my mom to live with us, and Dwight was a good friend of the family. He was one of the most gentle, quiet and kind people I ever knew.

Dwight had known me since I was born. Violent fighting was way out of character for him. I jumped out of my bed in my underclothes, dashed down the hallway, and ran down the stairs, through the kitchen and out the door. Lonnie was almost dead; he had no fight left in him. Still, Dwight kept hitting him with some of the hardest blows I ever saw.

Lonnie was lifeless as blood covered his face. He wasn't breathing and his body was as limp as a dead snake. With no shirt and no shoes, I ran straight out into ten inches of snow and shouted at the top of my lungs, "Dwight, stop!" Immediately, Dwight stopped hitting Lonnie. Dwight suddenly became very apologetic both to me and to my mother. I picked up Lonnie and dragged his lifeless body into the house. He was bleeding profusely, trailing thick blood to the couch. I began cleaning his face with a damp towel. My mom and I did all we could do to stop the bleeding.

I looked Dwight in his saddened eyes filled with regret and said to him, "Dwight, you have to go."

"Mikey, I'm sorry," he said as he gathered his things to leave. Then he looked at my mother and said, "Sandy, I'm sorry. I will never do that again." He tried to explain that Lonnie had been disrespecting my mother. He couldn't sit there and let him say the things he was saying to her.

"Mikey, your mother is like a sister to me, and I will never let anyone hurt her."

My mother took a long time to make sure the blood was

off of Lonnie's face. Afterward, I locked up the doors and went back to bed.

The next morning, I got up and went to school like nothing ever happened. I had to go to school just to get some peace. That was my life and it was really starting to take its toll on me. My siblings were also affected by the things we had to go through.

Through all of that violence and chaos, I wondered about my dad. Where was he? I knew that if he were there, I wouldn't have had to be the man of the house as a child. But I did my best to always make sure my brothers and sister felt a sense of security. I made sure they were in bed before I was. I would watch over them as I slept with one eye open and one eye closed. But there was no way to know what was going to happen at our house. In short, my childhood was constantly a "hell in the cell" wrestling match.

The winter was cold. There was no insulation in our walls and frigid air from the cold night leaked through the cracks of the old wooden windows and floors. All four boys crammed in a twelve-by-ten foot room. We shared blankets, and half of the time we stuffed pillowcases with clothes to use for pillows. Staying warm was our main objective.

On multiple occasions, we had neither gas nor electricity. It soon became second nature to keep our food outside covered with snow to keep it cold. We managed to survive some of the coldest winters back then. I remember using a portable heater that barely heated up one room. To offset the chill, we even used my mother's heating pads that had been prescribed to her earlier from the local doctor's office. Those heating pads were often the only thing that kept us warm during the long winter nights.

All of us took advantage of the warmth of the school building. We also were able to eat breakfast and lunch there. It didn't matter what was on the menu, either. Being picky about food was not in our vocabulary. Picky eaters quickly learned that they could give me any of the food they didn't want.

For us, going to school was a safe haven, regardless of any drama or fights that broke out there. We saw and heard gunshots and fights all the time, so the petty affairs of high school students didn't matter much to me. I actually found school drama humorous compared to the unpredictable reality of life at home. I dreaded getting off the school bus. In fact, I made sure I sat in the back of the bus, gazing at the scenery as long as I could.

We hardly ever had video games, cable or even a phone. We couldn't relate to being entertained with cable TV. We certainly didn't have board games to pass the time during inclement weather. But then my Aunt Dorothy Jean moved to Columbus. She showed up one day with her south-side-of-Chicago accent saying, "I'm your Aunt Dorothy Jean." She visited us often, and when she did, she spent hours upon hours playing solitaire. I never learned how to play it and never wanted to, either. Aunt Dorothy Jean was obsessed with that game. She had a good time playing, too, laughing and joking all by herself.

Aunt Dorothy Jean was a very nice and giving person. She always made me feel special. She seemed to have enough money, too, and maybe that's why my mother enjoyed her company so much. Aunt Dorothy Jean would give me five dollars and I thought I was "the man" having that much money.

Every time she came over, her attitude completely transformed the atmosphere of our gloomy environment. She always greeted us with a kiss and said, "That's my baby." If she didn't take the time to show us how to play card games, she and my mother watched *The Five Heartbeats* again and again. That movie made me sick. They seemed to watch it at least once a day.

Whenever Aunt Dorothy Jean left, she always left a deck of cards. We were very creative with those cards, building dream houses and playing "match." As I got older, I learned how to play some adult games, too, but never solitaire.

Lost Hope for Brighter Days

Many nights I stared at the ceiling, hoping that the next day would be brighter. I was getting to the point in my life where I was losing faith in any change happening for us.

Still, I tried my best to be obedient, but obedience wasn't getting me anywhere. I wanted to leave, but I didn't have anywhere to go. My siblings had the same look in their eyes. Their dad would still make cameo appearances at the house, but he wasn't there enough to help raise them. He certainly wasn't dependable, and my siblings finally became immune to his tactics. He wasn't as well-received by his children as he once was. It seemed like he came to our house only to get a vacation from his other girlfriends. In fact, if Big Marv would have fully committed to making a family with us, I'm not sure if I would be writing this book.

Week after week, day after day, life was the same old and outdated humdrum. I was tired of getting cussed out, and I was tired of dope fiends. I was tired of drug dealers, and I was tired of living in roach and rat infested homes. I was tired of having hardly anything to eat after the first week of the month was over, and I was tired of being broke.

My wardrobe was horrible. None of us had many clothes to wear. When we were blessed to get anything new, it wasn't something off the store shelf. "New" for us was simply defined as something we didn't have before. We knew we had to hold on to our clothes so they could be passed down to the next brother and then to the next brother.

I was tired of being neglected, and I was tired of not having a girlfriend because of the clothes I had to wear. Even when I did have a crush on someone who I really liked, I was too shy and embarrassed to talk to her because I knew my home life was so messed up. I would have made a good boyfriend to a girl, though. I was always the type of guy to do all I could for someone when I cared for that person. But I wasn't willing to risk pulling a girlfriend into the life I lived.

During this time I was still a virgin, too. I feared having a baby or catching an STD. Plus, even though I didn't know who my father was, I knew he had other children scattered all over. My mother told me that I had sisters, but for some reason she couldn't remember their names. There was no telling what they looked like. I was scared to fall hard for a girl and then find out she was my sister. I wanted to be married and in love before I had sex, anyway, even though being a virgin was very unpopular. To me, being in a committed relationship only brought unnecessary problems, and I had enough issues outside of school. Besides, I saw how seriously guys took their girlfriends. It was tempting, though, and my school had some of the most beautiful young women that I had ever seen. But I knew it would be risky, so I became more like a brother than a lover. I needed school to stay my safe haven, not be my battleground.

Still, I never felt like I could get close to anybody. I was a good kid, and those who really knew me back then knew I wasn't a troublemaker, although at times I could be troublesome. I had school friends for the most part, but that's where it stopped for me. We had too many problems, and bringing people into our home wasn't a risk I was willing to take. So, I kept my "school friends" at school.

We'd play ball together or I'd cut their hair. Some guys really liked the haircuts I gave and they became faithful clients. Giving haircuts is how I earned money to care for my sister and brothers. During the first through the fifth of the month, we normally had plenty of food. But after that, food became scarce. It didn't really matter much if we were hungry. If we didn't have food, we didn't have food. Keeping my haircut money away from my mother helped to offset those hungry days in the month. I even had to hide my money in the sole of my shoe, because my mother would take it otherwise. I couldn't let her take my money. I refused to support the alcohol and drug habits that infested my family. My mother never believed me when I told her I had no money, and she would search through my room and my clothes. I finally decided that it was safer to go to my clients' homes or take my clippers to school. I'd cut hair in the locker room, band room, or anywhere other than my house just to be able to keep my money.

Dee was my main client, and he was very picky about his hair. He would not let anyone cut his hair except me. I grew up with Dee in my old neighborhood and we kept in touch even after I had moved. He was one of my only friends who understood my situation. In fact, he faced some of the same struggles I faced. He was planning on moving out on his own once he became of age.

Whenever he would come over, my mother didn't mind me going off with him for a few hours, and sometimes she even let me spend the night at his house. He could read the frustration in my face, and that allowed me to vent to him about my life, particularly things that were going on at home. The closer he got to getting his own apartment, he would tell me, "If your mother keeps tripping on you, you can come and live with me." I understood him loud and clear, and I was going to hold him to his word if I needed him. But the very thought of leaving Marvin, Fee, Rodney and JD made me sad. So, I tucked his offer in the back of my mind.

HOOP DREAMS

Basketball was all I had as an escape. I remember going up to Cleo Dumaree Athletic Complex, also referred to as Nelson's gym. That favorite hangout was made up of four collegiate-sized basketball courts. A host of other leagues played there including the Nike League, and AAU tournaments and tryouts were hosted there, too. Everybody played ball at Nelson. Since it only took me five minutes to walk there, I was at Nelson every chance I could get. I watched the Ohio State University basketball players play open gym, and I got to see great players there like Jimmy Jackson and

Esteban Weaver.

I loved being at Nelson, watching and learning from so many great players. I watched all their moves and how they played offense and defense. Then I'd try to adopt their moves for myself. Every so often, I would have the opportunity to play with some of the guys and I tried to play my best. I was motivated, and I would shoot around in an open court until my opportunity came. If there weren't any open courts inside, I would go to the outside courts and work on my game unless they were outside playing. If they were, then I would wait to see who had "next."

"I GOT NEXT," I would say, courageously.

We all had dreams of one day becoming professional athletes, and most of the time, we played ball from dusk to dawn. Playing basketball was an everyday thing, and it kept my mind off the problems I faced at home.

I had a real goal: I wanted to play ball for my high school. I knew the competition was going to be fierce and that made me work even harder. I didn't receive much favoritism, either; I just had to flat-out earn success. I had been an underdog all my life, whether it was on the basketball court, wrestling team, marching band, jazz band, football team, chess club, or even having to defend myself against the reigning class clown of the school, Jawanza Moore. Having to earn all of my stripes wasn't foreign to me at all. It was normal for me to fight for everything I wanted.

I had a chip on my shoulder and something to prove. After all, I had earned the "Most Improved Player of The Year Award" as a sophomore. I knew I was just as good if not better than most of the players on the team. Since I was new to the school, though, I had to earn every minute I got.

At the beginning of the season, our coach had already pre-selected his starters. I wasn't included in the coach's initial plans, but I worked as hard as I could in every practice. The coach clearly still had his favorites, but the team knew that I was good enough to be a starter. I stayed diligent and continued to work on my game. I studied every player on the team, and I knew their strengths and weaknesses. When the first team would scrimmage the second team, I did my best to show the coach that I was a good player by holding my own against his favorites.

Finally, a few of the starters didn't have the grades to play during the second half of the season. My number was called and the coach had no choice but to use me. And I delivered. I played point guard and ran the offense. I also made sure I gave the ball to the scorers in their sweet spots.

During my academic and athletic highs, I never had any family support whatsoever. But I learned to mask my pain. It wasn't hard for me to put a smile on my face or crack jokes with fellow class clowns. Most of my peers had no idea what life was like for me and my family. Periodically, my frustration from home would leak into my school day, resulting in a bad day in class or even a detention. But overall, I wasn't a troublemaker. Every so often, I would get into small conflicts, but they didn't result in any altercations. I knew if I got suspended I would have to be at home, so I did my best to stay out of the kind of trouble that would keep me home for any length of time. People respected me because I was respectful to them. For the most part, I loved going to school. It had its perks, especially getting to eat breakfast and lunch. I definitely couldn't chance wasting any meals.

Out of the Eagle's Nest

One thing I hated was hearing my youngest brother, JD, cry for Mommy. Half of the time there was nothing wrong with him, either. One of the things my mother wouldn't tolerate was for anyone to correct JD. When he was younger, he made sure to tell my mother if he wasn't getting his way, and he had the most irritating cry.

"Mommy! Mikey won't fix me a sandwich or some powdered milk!" he would cry in his familiar chant. Whatever he wanted, that's what he cried about. Then my mother would get irritated about his crying. Even though we were poor, JD somehow managed to get whatever he wanted within the confines of what we had available. That got on everybody's nerves. When nobody was around, lil' Marv and Rodney would make JD pay for acting like that. Rodney would rough him up with a few punches and slams, especially if my mother wasn't around to punish him.

One evening I had to put JD in his place for acting up. As soon as he screamed and cried, the floor began shaking and the steps got closer and closer as my mother marched down the hall. She looked at me with a mean glare and yelled, "Get out!"

I looked at Marv, Fee, Rodney and JD. They were very sad because they knew I was leaving for good. My mind was already made up before I gathered my things into a black trash bag. I even believe my mother knew I wasn't coming back. She didn't change her mind, either, and she didn't call me back into the house after I left. So, I walked to a pay-phone and paged Dee with our secret code we had agreed to use if this happened. I waited by the phone until he called me back, which took less than a minute. I told him what happened, and he told me to meet him at his apartment. It was about a ten or fifteen minute walk and it was freezing cold outside. I made haste and got to Dee's as quickly as I could.

Years later, my sister Fee told me she remembered that day like it was yesterday. She said that my mother told people that I ran away. Fee also said that while I was walking down the street, she ran outside yelling my name, but I didn't respond. I just kept walking. Truthfully, I didn't hear anyone calling me–maybe because I was in tears. My mind just recited over and over my mother's words: "Get out!"

Fee didn't want me to go. In fact, leaving my siblings was one of my most hurtful moments. I knew that leaving would bring some severe repercussions on all of them. I worried for their safety. But being the "man of the house" was too much pressure.

At that point, looking back wasn't an option any more. The road ahead was bleak. I was only sixteen and I was forced to walk in the shoes of a man.

I wondered where my dad was. If he were there, maybe I could have moved in with him. But he wasn't there. The world ahead of me was nothing but a white-out, and it seemed like I would have to fight through the blizzard alone.

FRIENDS TO THE END

I met my best friend Ryan in the fourth grade, and since then, we were inseparable. We formed one of the greatest friendships that, in my opinion, God would allow. Ryan and I were in contact almost every day for years, and the people who knew us would say the same thing. For the most part, my story is his story because we spent so much time together.

I was really blessed to be considered a part of their family, and they treated me like I was one of their own. I called his grandma, "Grandma," his uncles, "Uncle," his aunts, "Aunt" and his cousins were my cousins. The same went for him and my family and siblings. I also was able to capture a clear picture of how I thought a father should be, and I used Ryan's father as the measuring stick on how fathers should treat their sons.

Ryan's parents had separated when he was young, but

Ryan and his father, Mr. Jon, spent lots of time together–quality time. They would have two or three-hour conversations about whatever. They'd play Nintendo, chess and do a plethora of other activities.

Mr. Jon was a great chess player, and over time, Ryan became a better and better player, too.

He lost many matches against his father, but he never gave up. After each loss, he'd replay each move in his mind. He studied his father's signature move while developing counter-attacks of his own. Ryan's level of focus and determination, coupled with his relentless attitude, made him a more reputable competitor. Meanwhile, his father didn't have any peers to sharpen his iron. Ryan and I played against each other for hours upon hours preparing for the ultimate competitor–Mr. Jon.

I remember the day he beat his father fair and square. It was the happiest day of Ryan's little life up to that point, and the sense of accomplishment was major. I was happy for him, too, as if I was the one who had beaten Mr. Jon.

Ryan and his father would go fishing and I'd watch them interact with each other. Mr. Jon helped maneuver his son's fingers on the fishing rod, and he taught his son how to tie his hook on the end of his fishing line. The two of them didn't always agree, and Ryan didn't always obey, but he knew who his father was.

Sometimes, Ryan shared how he felt when he'd be

angry at his dad. He often complained that when he really needed his father to be his hero, he never suited up. To me, Ryan's dad looked like the ideal father. Since I didn't understand the complexities of the situation, I was stubborn about Ryan's accusations. He had a very tough upbringing, especially on his mother's side of his family. His father's side of the family seemingly had more structure in terms of morals and values. I believe that was mainly because of the family pillar: *Grandma*.

Grandma created a family culture full of tradition and unity like I had never seen before in my life. Even though Grandma lived in one of the roughest neighborhoods in Columbus, it was home to her and she had lived there for over twenty years. She didn't seem to have many friends, but she had family and that was where her heart was. Grandma literally raised three generations. When family needed a place to stay, she was there, no matter what was going on in their lives. She always welcomed them with open arms. Grandma fixed some of the best meals, too. She would sit us down, look us straight in the eyes, and tell us the truth.

Ryan and his sister Erika stayed with Grandma for long periods of time. Ryan and Erika were very close, and no matter what she was doing he'd make sure she was safe. They lived at Grandma's house for years. Living with Grandma required that they did their chores and be in the house by curfew. Ryan's dad stayed with Grandma, too, and I'm not sure of the reason. I was never bold enough to ask him. Ryan told me they were all staying there due to the living conditions of their mother's house. Only until I met his mother was I able to understand, and I didn't meet her until several years into my blooming friendship with Ryan.

I still couldn't understand how Ryan could have such issues with his father. It sounded to me like his mother's situation was the real issue. I would sit and listen to Ryan share with me hours upon hours of stories about life with his mom. He had a whole different set of friends over at his mother's house, and drugs and alcohol had invaded there, too. Ryan's stories were horrific. In fact, Ryan had many sleepless nights replaying in his mind some of the beatdowns his mother took. Even though Ryan stayed in a safe haven and had comfort provided at Grandma's house, he constantly worried about the safety of his mother. The guy she was with at the time was vicious, and he'd hit her like she was a man who stole something from him. His mother was often left bruised, battered, and scarred. Ryan and Erika would tremble in fear, listening from another room as their mother screamed. Screams and cries reverberated throughout their home. Ryan and Erika saw their mother being beaten while drugs, alcohol, crime and violence took over their home. Ryan often quoted the late Tupac Shakur when he talked about life at his mother's house: "I'm going to get my weight up with my hate and pay him back when I'm bigger."

I always wondered why women who suffered from domestic violence go back to the person who provided such an uncompromising relationship. It is something that I may never understand. It's like a mother bear traveling peacefully through the woods:

She maneuvers through the forest ducking and dodging tree branches. She feels the cool breeze brushing her face. Suddenly, she finds herself trapped by her ankle, in agonizing pain. She does all she can to cope with the pain until she figures out how to break loose from the trap. Once she breaks free, her basic instincts tell her to travel through the woods a different way. In fact, that bear makes sure to avoid that dangerous path altogether. The bear even becomes more cautious with each step until she gets to a place of safety, especially after her safety has been compromised. And if that bear sees another trap, she is sure to avoid it completely.

Bears are strong animals by nature. Women are strong, too, and I don't know why Ryan's mother stayed with that man who abused her. I knew what addiction and drug violence did to families, and I knew they were traps in and of themselves. But I had no understanding as to why a mother would trade her entire family in exchange for horrible beatings. It's extremely damaging for children to watch their mother take beating after beating after beating, and then watch her go back to the trap again and again. I'm not sure what goes on in the mind of an abuser, but I saw what the violence did to Ryan and Erika, and I knew what drug violence in my house had done to me.

Living in the structured environment with Grandma caused conflict within Ryan's soul. He wanted his father to go protect his mother and keep her safe the same way he kept him and Erika safe. Ryan wanted to be with his mother to help protect her, but there was an internal struggle to keep himself out of danger, too. How can a little boy choose between his own safety or his mother's?

So, those were Ryan's issues with his dad. He had "superhero" dreams of his dad busting down the door and defeating the evil villain with one punch in the chest. The villain would be hit so hard that he would fly into outer space. Ryan needed his dad to protect him and his family from danger.

Ryan further explained that some of those horrific events he experienced were matters of life and death. Calling the police only made matters worse, and it actually intensified the situation. The only person he felt should have been there was his father, which created a deep level of resentment inside of Ryan. I'm not sure if his father fully understood where his son's anger stemmed.

As Ryan continued to grow and develop, his life had a thick line dividing what he learned while living with his father, from what he learned while living with his mother. The challenge for him was finding a happy medium because he had a heart that was full of love and compassion for those he loved. It was hard for him simply because of the neighborhoods where we grew up. I spent more time with Ryan than anybody, and I saw how hard he tried. But the crack epidemic hit his mother's home as well as mine. The chaos it caused was residual.

Throughout his life, Ryan couldn't fully decide if he wanted to be an upstanding citizen or a hustler. Ryan was involved in two different worlds at the same time, and each world offered totally different results. I saw that he wanted better, but his level of exposure had already had too much of a negative impact on his life. For much of his early years, all Ryan saw was people getting drunk and high without any regard for going to work or being a strong influence in their families. Through certain periods he wanted to be a thug, and then at other times he wanted to settle down, get married and have children. Sometimes he wanted to get a job and go back to school, and other times he wanted to hit the streets and make fast money. Choosing the fast money always created conflict, but it seemed to be his choice by default. He started off wanting just to meet a basic need. Once the need was met, then Ryan had to come to the decision to quit hustling. By then, though, he had customers who relied on him to supply them with whatever he was selling. Ryan was highly celebrated by his peers, too. People absolutely loved him. When he walked into the room, the party started. And

I can't begin to describe the number of females who threw themselves at him. They were always fascinated by his light hazel eyes and sandy brown curly hair. They would fight to meet him. They even went behind each other's backs just to have a chance with him.

Whenever Ryan needed anything, all he had to do was make a quick phone call and he was in business. That was the street way. Once he built momentum and large quantities of cash were flowing in every day, it became very hard for him to stop. The partying and staying up all night sucked a person right into the street life. As a result, he really never escaped the pattern of abuse he saw during his childhood.

Every so often he and I would get in disagreements that would last too long for us, so we would fight each other, but we never threw any punches. We didn't want to hurt each other. Still, we both knew those were not fair and square fights.

I was pretty good at wrestling since I wrestled for two years in high school. I also wrestled when I was younger in the rec league. Ryan had no experience in wrestling, so I had a major advantage. I knew moves and holds that created discomfort for him. His pride wouldn't let him lose, though, so he would grab my genitals and squeeze, which put me in agonizing pain. My pride wouldn't allow me to let go, either, so I would apply pressure and cut off his circulation. But still, neither one of us would let go. We could hold like that for at least an hour stalemate when we fought. And we never let others see us fight because we wanted to make it seem like we were cool all the time.

"If you let me go, I'll let you go," we'd say to each other. We were both cautious. If we didn't get the timing right, then the other one would have the advantage, making the standoff last longer. Those few moments were the only moments of our bond where we didn't trust each other.

Ryan and I had small pockets of disconnection due to relocation, whether it was him moving back with his mother or my family moving to a different side of town. We always kept in contact on some level, though, even when I was couch-surfing. For the most part, he knew my whereabouts. If I needed him to keep a secret, he did. Even though I became incognito as far as my family was concerned, I knew it wouldn't be hard for Ryan to find me.

THE UNDERGROUND HELL ROAD

After my mother kicked me out, I couch-surfed as long as anyone would give me a place to lay my head. I slept on the couch or on the floor, and people went out of their way to help me. I was a young man who didn't have a plan–a young man who didn't know if his next meal was going to come. But I was always taught that "a closed mouth don't get fed."

My friend Dee took me in for a while. My time with

Dee could easily be a book in and of itself. Dee had a big heart, but at the same time he would tell people exactly how he felt, no matter how his comments were received. Dee was drug and alcohol-free like I was, mainly because he also saw how drugs affected his family and friends. He never wanted to let those things influence his decisions.

Dee and I had more good times than bad times, and we were more like brothers than friends. In fact, when people first met us, they thought exactly that. It wasn't because we looked alike, but rather because of our interactions. We'd fuss and argue over some of the smallest things and then laugh about it later. Our birthdays were even on the same day, but he was a year older. Dee had a very hard time trusting people and I was one of the few people he trusted. He was very loyal, too, and he was looking for the same loyalty in return. For some reason he had a strong, family kind of love toward me, and I felt the same way about him.

Dee's apartment was a one-bedroom on the corner of Bulen and Livingston Avenue. I slept on the couch until he got a bunk bed for me and other friends who would sleep over. He was a neat freak and a germaphobe, too. If I didn't clean my mess, we had problems–his house, his rules. He also had nice clothes and shoes, and we wore the same size. Even though I was taller than he was, he'd buy his clothes big so we could share. We'd spend a lot of time riding in his 1981 Cadillac Coupe Deville. Dee had a fetish for Cadi's.

I wasn't working at the time, so he had to pay all of the bills. I continued going to school and focused on trying to get my diploma so I could go to college. Dee encouraged this.

Even though I kept going to school, my mother wanted me to come home. She even came to my school and did all she could do to find me. I stayed far away from anybody who would tell my mother my whereabouts. I knew I was stubborn–just like my mom. I told myself I wasn't going back, no matter what.

My mother then called the school attendance office where the varsity basketball coach spent most of his mornings. If I was in school that day, my mother would ask to speak to me, and the office would send for me. The first time this happened, I had no idea why the attendance office wanted me. I knew I wasn't in any trouble because I was truly doing my best academically. I wasn't going to let my grades be the reason I couldn't play ball.

When I walked into the office, I was told that my mother was on the phone and she wanted to talk to me. I knew my mother was up to something. She may have had issues, but she was very clever. I scanned the room, trying to read the faces of the office staff. I wasn't sure what my mother may have already told them.

But as soon as I picked up the phone, my mother started screaming and hollering at me, slaying me with cuss words and yelling for me to come home. I made sure I pressed the phone receiver hard to my ear to cut down on the sound. The office was quiet enough as it was, and I couldn't let the staff hear my business. I kept a calm, straight face and spoke to my mom like nothing was going on.

"Well, that's what the coach thought," I told her, which had nothing to do with what she was screaming. I just pretended we were having a normal conversation. She kept yelling and I kept pretending like she was checking on me. The office staff could only hear my end of the conversation anyway.

Suddenly, my mother said, "I sent the police after you, and they are on their way."

"Thanks, Mom. I love you, too," I said, and I hung up. The office staff didn't have a clue that there was a problem. I thanked the staff and walked out of the office to head to class. Suddenly, I saw two officers heading toward the office. I instantly got tense, so I did what I was taught in the marching band: I quickly did an about-face and walked to the other end of the hall like everything was fine. Then, as soon as I got to the corner of the hall, I turned and ran as fast as I could. I made it to a phone booth and paged Dee, putting in my code to meet him at our designated place. Any time that happened I ended up missing at least a week of school until I knew things had cooled off.

A Father's Love

Meanwhile, I reconnected with an old girlfriend named Angie. She was very special to me, and she was very shy. I met her while we were in middle school, but never really connected outside of that until we were older. Our interactions were mainly by phone, and sometimes I was able to sit on the porch at her house. When I lived at home with my mother, we hardly ever had consistent phone service. That made it challenging to talk to anyone. But Angie and I had spurts when we talked, and then weeks would pass before we had any contact at all.

By the time we reconnected, Angie was attending Brookhaven High School. Her parents had four daughters and no sons, and they kept a close eye on their girls. Angie lived in a two-parent home, and her father was a protective, no-nonsense kind of guy. When I had the opportunity to go see her, we sat on their screened-in porch and talked. It felt good to talk to a female. I knew she would listen to me and give me good advice. We were very comfortable with each other, and I needed somebody I could trust.

Angie started hanging out with me at Dee's. It got to a point where she didn't want to leave. She began to cut school and it quickly got out of hand. Soon, she was cutting school over and over again. It got to the point where she didn't even try to go home at 3:30 p.m. when the school day was over for everyone else. I made many attempts to persuade her to go home, but she just wouldn't go. I knew her parents were worried and that they would be looking for her. Besides, I always thought her father was crazy. To make matters worse, we were both virgins until she started spending so much time with me at Dee's. Making Angie's dad mad was not on my list of things to do. It took about a month, and I don't know how her father found out where Dee lived, but he did. He even threatened to send the police if Angie didn't come out.

I have to give her dad credit. He came for his daughter and he didn't let anything stop him. I can't imagine what it would be like to have my dad fight for me like that. As it was, the only person I had trying to get me back was my mother, but eventually she gave up trying to get me to come home.

Nevertheless, Angie did go home and it hurt for a while. I also understood that Angie and I handled things totally wrong. I should have been more respectful and honored her father enough to knock on his door. I should have asked him if I could take his daughter to the movies or something. Instead, we made decisions without proper consent from her parents.

Angie and I were over, and her dad made sure that we would never see each other again. For some reason, I respected his feelings and I pulled back. The life I was living wasn't safe anyway. Anything could have happened at any time. Plus, I broke my own rule by bringing someone into my life when I knew I was living in an unstable and unpredictable situation.

VAL

Dee had a friend named Val, whom he considered a little sister. He had known her for years, ever since the Gardens.

There was something very different about Val, though. She was very smart and she did really well in school. Val definitely was ahead of her time in wisdom. She was not only respected, but she was loved in her community. She brought smiles to everyone in her path, and she naturally peer-mediated all kinds of situations. She was also rowdy and she had a big mouth, too.

Val was already in a relationship, according to Dee. I had no intentions of getting with her anyway, and she felt the same way about me. Over time, though, Val and I became really good friends. After a while Dee took interest in Sarah, one of Val's friends who lived in a nicer part of town. For some reason, Val's mother had no problem allowing her to hang out with me, Sarah, and Dee all weekend long.

Dee and Sarah formed an intimate relationship and they took full advantage of Val's mother's trust. Their intimate experiences lasted all weekend and often into the week itself. Soon, whenever the girls came over, Sarah and Dee went off together and Val and I ended up taking walks by ourselves.

We spent lots of time just talking.

One weekend, Dee encouraged me to see Val differently. I took note of his words and eventually, Val and I took our relationship to the next level. We started dating and things got serious, but Val was still a virgin. Although many guys at her school and in her neighborhood did all they could to be her first, she had held her ground.

But then Val and I wanted to become intimately involved. It wasn't easy. My sexual experience was very limited. I had only been with Angie. It took Val and me months of trying everything I thought I knew. This caused us to spend even more time with each other, even after Dee and Sarah tapered off. Val and I had fun and it was also nice to know that her mother approved of us spending time together.

One night, Dee, Sarah, Val and I were sitting under a light on a green electrical transformer box. We were out in the Gardens near Val's house, laughing and joking. Out of nowhere, two guys walked up on us with guns aimed our way. One guy had two 9mms and the other guy had a twelve-gauge pump shotgun. One false move would have cost us our lives. I was gunless, but Dee had a gun on him. In fact, he had a two-shooter, a small .22 handgun.

The two guys were very aggressive and they started interrogating us about someone else who lived in the Gardens. I was scared. I had seen so much in my life. So many people died as victims of the streets. Of course, Val and Sarah were horrified, but for some reason, Dee felt the need to talk tough with these guys–with only a two-shooter on him. He barely had enough bullets to save himself. I knew the rest of us didn't have a chance. Dee and I told them we had nothing to do with the person they wanted. Shortly thereafter they left us and continued their hunt. As soon as they got out of our view, we quickly went somewhere safe.

I was impressed with Val in that situation. I could see that even though she was scared, she was tough and she knew how to survive. This brought us even closer, and as time progressed, we got even closer still. Throughout all this, though, her father was nowhere to be found. He could have come through like Angie's dad, sweeping in and hauling her away from "bad influences" like me and Dee. Dee needed his father, too, but he was nowhere to be found, either.

Where were the fathers?

IMPOSTER

It was graduation night, and parties were everywhere. I was hitting all of the parties. It seemed like the entire Walnut Ridge student body was at every one of them, celebrating all of the seniors who graduated. There were enough parties in my area that I was able to walk to them all. We had a blast enjoying the cookouts, music and dancing.

By the time I headed back to Dee's house, it was late. I

unlocked the door, but the chain lock stopped the door from opening. I knew something had to be up; it was not like Dee to do that. I began to listen through the door. To my surprise, I heard Angie's voice.

"Stop touching me!" I heard her say.

I went to the window in the back alley and yelled through the screen. When he heard me, Dee stopped doing whatever he was attempting to accomplish that night. I got inside and Angie ran behind me. Dee and I began to argue. It took everything in me not to start swinging on him. He must have seen the look in my eyes. Then he pulled a gun out on me. I knew he wasn't going to shoot me, but I wasn't going to test him. He told me to get out, so I grabbed my things and left, taking Angie with me. We started to walk toward the nearest payphone, which was about two blocks away.

At that point, my thoughts were all over the place. It was too much to handle and my adrenaline had peaked.

What just happened? I thought. *Did Dee just pull a gun on me? We could have handled it fair and square–duked it out like two boxers. Why did Angie even risk coming back after all the things that transpired earlier with her father? I trusted Dee like a brother. I thought he and I were better than that. Now what? Where do I go from here? I have no-where to go. It's past midnight. Who's going to let me in this late in the evening?*

Angie and I walked as fast as we could to the nearest

payphone so we could call a taxi for her. Despite my own problems, my first focus was getting her home safely. The taxi pulled up about fifteen minutes later. We said our good-byes as she slowly arranged herself in the back seat of the cab. With tears in her eyes she looked out the window at me. Her eyes said, "This is it… I may never see you again." I was sad, but relieved at the same time because that just wasn't the life for her. Moving on was a must, and the damage had been done. The cab faded in the distance and suddenly I realized I had nowhere to go. A night of celebrating for others became a night of clamor and turmoil for Angie, and a night of loss for me. I was on the road again.

BEYOND THE COMFORT ZONE

I walked down the street with nowhere to go, carrying most of my belongings (including my hair clippers) in a thirty-gallon trash bag. Suddenly, I remembered my friend Dale. He knew my situation. His parents had told me long ago that if I ever needed a place to stay, I could live with them. So I contacted Dale, and his parents remained true to their word.

In order for me to live there, though, Dale's parents required me to find a job. So I found a job as a parking lot security guard at the Midland building downtown. I gave Dale's parents fifty dollars out of each paycheck. In return, they provided me with a twin-sized bed and all my meals. They were very good to me and their family was close. Dale had three brothers and two cousins who stayed there along with his father and stepmother. Dale's family also did things differently than I did growing up. They all ate at the table as a family and someone would say grace before each dinner.

They also had family meetings to discuss whatever the issues were at hand.

Things were going well. I kept playing ball every day during the summer. I also worked out every day before and after work.

Val and I stayed connected, too, and we spent time with each other whenever we could. Then, Val told me that she was pregnant. There was no doubt in my mind that she was pregnant with my baby. I went to Dale's parents to tell them what was going on. Pops was supportive, but Dale's stepmother was very upset. Until then, I thought that evil stepmothers only existed in fairy tales and goodnight stories. But Dale's stepmother was very controlling and manipulative. We all knew that she was a ticking time bomb, and we constantly walked on eggshells around her.

One night they all had a family meeting about me, and I overheard the conversation. Dale's stepmother was very forceful with her words. She wanted me out of their house and wanted me out right then. That's when she called me upstairs and said, "You have to leave." Then, she instructed Dale to drop me off any place I wanted–just one place and then he had to come home. I packed my bag, gave my thanks, and said my goodbyes to everyone.

Places for me to go were limited, and I still couldn't be where my mom could reach me. I had to focus. Where could I go? Who would take me in? Dale was instructed to take me to only one place and he had a certain amount of time to drop me off. Once he got to the destination, I was on my own. I knew I could go back to Dee, even though he'd probably never let me back. I most definitely was not going home. I could go over to Aunt Phil's, but I knew my mom would end up finding out and she would hunt me down. All of a sudden, I thought of Ryan. Perhaps Aunt Sally (Ryan's aunt) would let me stay with them. Ryan was over at Grandma's with the rest of the family when I called. I directed Dale to take me to Grandma's.

When I got to Grandma's, Ryan and I huddled up outside like Phil Jackson drawing up a play for Kobe to take the last shot. I only had one chance to convince Aunt Sally to let me come. Ryan said, "Mike, I can tell you what to say, but I can't say it for you. You have to ask her yourself."

"What do I say?" I asked him.

"Tell her you spoke to me, and I told you I could get you a job at Hometown Buffet where I work. Also, offer to pay her fifty dollars every two weeks and that should work."

"You think she'll let me?" I asked.

"What's the worst a person can say?" he said.

Ryan was right. I prepared for a *no*, but expected a *yes*.

The clock was ticking, and Aunt Sally was about to pack everyone into her Honda Accord and hit the road. I pulled myself together. Besides, I just knew that Aunt Sally wouldn't let me live back out on the streets. Ryan stood off to the side, just far enough away so he could hear, but not close enough to be in our conversation.

I was very jittery when I approached Aunt Sally, but I shook off the jitters. I told her what had happened, and I also told her what Ryan instructed me to say. She thought about it for a moment. I waited and waited. She was looking at me while she processed and assessed the situation. I gave her my best sad face, complete with puppy dog eyes. Then she looked at me and said, "You better have my money," and she hugged me. I couldn't thank her enough! I turned and looked at Ryan. He smiled.

I was a man of my word, and I did everything I said I was going to do. Ryan was also a man of his word, and he got me a job working with him. When I needed him the most, he came through. There is nothing like having a friend like Ryan. We were like Jonathan and David in the Bible. Their souls were knitted and no one could change that. We were soul brothers.

I can't say things were always peaches and cream living at Aunt Sally's, but it was far away from the hood. I often wondered how my mom, Marvin, Fee, Rodney and JD were doing. In fact, I thought about them all the time. I dreamed and hoped that they were all right. In the meantime, Val was pregnant with our child, and I was still going to school. That was when Ryan found out that his girlfriend was pregnant, too. It was a lot for both of us. I decided to keep my focus on my academics and on playing ball. In my mind, I still had a chance to make it and be a good father to my baby.

I did everything I could do to stay focused and remain drug free. It wasn't always easy. Ryan handled the pressure differently than I did, smoking marijuana with the rest of the crew every chance he got. They got tired of trying to sway me into smoking with them. I said no every time. I told them if I ever smoked or drank it would be because I chose to, and not because somebody chose it for me.

The Great Last Hope

Finally, basketball tryouts arrived, and I knew it would be my breakout year. We had a great team along with a very solid supporting cast. At tryouts, I was locked and loaded. I gave it my all. I had played in summer and fall leagues to stay in shape to make sure I was competitive with the talent that year. Basketball was my last hope–my way out. I knew I could go to college and play ball even if I had to play as a walk-on. I refused to take no for an answer.

The last day of tryouts was over, and the next day I was in the band room for my first period class. Suddenly, the head coach peeked in and asked to pull me out of class. I was excited, because anything that had to do with basketball was exciting. Once we were out in the hall, the coach said, "Sorry, but I have to cut you."

"What?!"

I was not only a starter, but I was easily one of the top three or four players in our school that year. I asked him why, but all he said was, "It was a hard decision." The coach could barely look me in the eyes and tell me what drew him to that conclusion. At that point, my whole world came tumbling down in an instant.

Basketball was the only thing keeping me from living a negative life. It was my great last hope and all I needed was an opportunity to showcase my skills. I couldn't understand how he could cut me. It was very unusual for him to cut one of his best players. Even if he didn't want to let me start, I was still good enough to sit on the bench. When the other players who made the team found out that I didn't make it, they were shocked.

"Yo, you are needed on this team, man," they said. They even went to the coach and told him that they would give up their spot on the roster if he would let me play. But the coach wouldn't budge.

"I made my decision, and that's final," he told them.

That broke me completely. The one thing I prepared for–the one thing that I had control over–had been stripped from me. Basketball was the only opportunity I had left. People couldn't believe that the coach didn't take me back. Even administrative staff, teachers, custodians, and alumni could not understand why the coach would make a move like that.

Later, I was in the car riding with Ryan and the rest of the crew while they were smoking marijuana. After all that time standing my ground, I caved.

"Pass it over here," I said to them. Their faces froze with disbelief.

"Are you sure?" they said.

"Yes, I'm sure. Pass it over here."

And that's where it began.

From that point on, my life was not where I hoped it would be. I made my way back into the old neighborhood. Eventually, I quit my job and moved back to the hood. That's when things went from bad to worse. There is a huge difference between growing up in the hood and living the street life. Just living in a rough neighborhood doesn't force a person to get involved in crime. It's a gradual process.

In the beginning, I still had resistance. I still had the power to say no to things that made me feel uncomfortable. But soon, things that were once abnormal became normal for me. I never intended to drink alcohol or smoke cigars, but the more time I spent in that environment, the more I got sucked in.

It was like being in the twilight zone, pulled into a new school of thought. I was soon surrounded by a group of teenagers and young adults who did exactly what they wanted to do. It wasn't uncommon to watch a toddler being taught how to cuss, or to see young kids hooked on cigarettes. It was common to see a teenage guy pull out large amounts of cash and tell everyone how he just made a thousand dollars in a matter of hours by selling crack. Right after he walked away, the same guys who celebrated with him plotted how they could rob him.

I found myself in a place I wasn't ready to be. The problem was I was "cool" with everyone: gang members, crooks, pimps, prostitutes, dope fiends, killers and hustlers. They were my "friends."

Ryan and I didn't want to live a life of crime, and we weren't going to become drug dealers. We were about to be fathers. We didn't want to go to jail or even get hurt in the streets. By then, we both had officially quit school, but we tried our best to stay away from trouble. Even though we dropped out, we landed jobs at McDonald's. One of our friends was a manager at the downtown location on the corner of Main Street and Grant. We started out making a little over four dollars per hour. We were fine with that, though, because we wanted anything to keep us off the streets. We had to be there for our girlfriends and kids.

It was daytime on March 20, 1996, and I heard that Val was getting ready to have the baby. I was petrified, confused, and jumbled. Me, a dad? What? I didn't know what to do. I didn't have a plan. I didn't even have my own place to stay. I was still couch-surfing. My nerves were bad, too, and the only thing I knew to calm myself down was to get high. I was so drunk and high that day, I missed my baby being born. In fact, I was passed out drunk on the floor at Ryan's mom's house. I didn't even make it to the hospital until the next day.

Val was infuriated with me. I didn't like making Val mad. She was my girl, my love and my heart. When she first told me she was pregnant, I told her that I would always be there for her. When her dad got wind that she was expecting a baby, he actually tried to make Val go to the abortion clinic. Val had no respect whatsoever for her dad. He was never there for her when she needed him. So I vowed to her that she would never have to worry about me not being there. And yet, I started off baby Mikekeila Dean's life by breaking my promise to her mother.

For some reason, Val got over it quickly, and we focused on our newborn baby. Still, Val kept a look in her eye that said, "I'm going to get you later." Since our daughter was premature, the doctors had to perform a C-section. That also meant that Val and the baby needed to stay in the hospital longer than expected. I was at the hospital with them day in and day out, along with a host of friends. I sat in a chair next to the bed and held our newborn daughter.

There was only one person missing from the picture: my mom. I wanted her there, but we hadn't talked in about a year-and-a-half. She didn't even know I had a baby. I missed my mom. Val's family was there to support us. Some of our friends and mutual friends were there supporting us, too. But my mom had missed out on one of the most memorable moments in our lives. Obviously, my dad was still nowhere to be found, and I still had never seen or even met him at that point. I couldn't help but wonder how it would be to have him there in the hospital with us.

Life went on, and I spent as much time as I could with Val to help her as she was healing from her surgery. I kept going to work because I needed money to take care of my family. But I soon found out that the money I had been making wasn't nearly enough to support a family. All of my money was accounted for when I got paid, plus I had to set aside a few dollars for my habits. Most of the McDonald's staff there smoked weed, and I can remember going on breaks by the dumpster in the back to take a few hits. We just did it to get through the workday.

Once my shift ended, we'd all meet at a friend's house. Most of the time, I was a closer, which meant I would bring bags of Big Macs, quarter pounders with cheese, apple pies and tons of other food. Depending on the mood I was in when I got to the hangout spot, I could sell the food, trade it for weed, or I'd give it away.

THE SPOT

Our hangout spot was the home of one of my good

friend's sister. The crew I was in had all-access, while at least four other crews also came and hung out there. Most of us had either dropped out or were on the verge of dropping out. We got high and gambled on anything from NBA Live to Mortal Kombat Ultimate. We'd even gamble to see whose crew would win in a basketball game or who could do the most push-ups.

In my crew when guys got mad at each other, someone would yell, "Let's put on the gloves!" This meant to put on the boxing gloves and go a few rounds. For the most part, the guys would make up afterward. Anyone who didn't accept the challenge lost by default, and losers got made fun of for a long time afterward. They were being judged from the moment they got called out. This was also a way to rank people within the crew. And yes, we kept score of how many good hits each person took. It was definitely better to accept the challenge and lose the match than it was to ditch the fight.

I remember one time one of the guys was playing Ryan in NBA Live on PS2. The guy and Ryan had a great relationship, but he was blowing Ryan to smithereens, all the while calling Ryan everything but a child of God. Ryan had pride issues like everyone else, and he said, "You call me that name one more time, you and I are putting on the gloves!" Ryan was boiling so hot, I could almost hear him sizzling.

At that point, Ryan didn't even care about the game any more. His face squeezed, his eyes were pressed and he couldn't wait for that guy to say one more wrong word. I watched Ryan closely after he made his challenge to the guy, but I couldn't help laughing. Everyone knew that something was going to happen. The guy was so focused on the game, he wasn't paying attention to Ryan at all. He slam-dunked another ball and called Ryan another name.

Without further conversation, Ryan put his gloves on and threw the other pair of gloves in the guy's lap. By that time, the rest of us were laughing so hard, tears were flowing from our eyes. The guy stood up and quickly tried to put his gloves on, but Ryan started launching missiles at his face before he was ready. The rest of us were on the floor laughing so hard that we couldn't breathe. Ryan kept hitting with some type of Mortal Kombat seven or eight-punch combination that left the guy dazed. Finally, Ryan took his gloves off and said, "Don't you ever disrespect me like that again, or next time we won't use any gloves!"

I made sure to keep Val away from that environment at all costs. As much fun as we had, things could get ugly real quick. Ryan and I were still working at McDonald's, doing the same routine almost every day. It was getting old, though, and the money wasn't good for all the long hours we were working.

I began to trade work for hanging out. I didn't want to quit working, and I wasn't trying to get deep in the street life, either, but one day it happened. Our crew didn't have as much money as all of the other crews. In fact, we were broke. I'm not sure how we even had money to finance our drinking and weed habits.

One day two of the guys in our crew came to the hangout spot with a wad of cash. "How did ya'll get that money?" Ryan and I asked them.

They told us they hooked up with some guys from Detroit. That's when we started calling them "The Detroit Boys." Ryan and I looked at each other.

"Can we get in?" we asked. We wanted to make money, too.

While I was still working at McDonald's, I tried to sell weed, but I wasn't successful. I kept getting high off my own supply, and this made my bags too small for people to want to purchase. People didn't see me as a dependable weed seller, either. Selling crack was looking to be a more realistic avenue, because I knew I wasn't going to put a crack pipe to my mouth.

They let the Detroit Boys know that we were interested in selling crack. One of the guys looked at the both of us and said, "This ain't McDonald's." We understood, and we were fine with that. I knew I was taking a big leap of faith. I was getting ready to do something that I had vowed within myself I would never do. I didn't know the first thing about being a crack dealer. Selling weed was one thing, but selling crack was something totally different. After vouching for us, though, our guys felt like the Detroit Boys would gladly give us an opportunity.

Ryan and I met with the Detroit Boys, who interviewed us. They were impressed. They knew that we were novices and that they wouldn't have to pay us at the rate of an experienced drug dealer.

THINGS GOT REAL

The Detroit Boys were older than we were. Smoke and G. were the two main guys. Smoke's name spoke for itself. I never witnessed a guy who stayed as high as he did. He had a cool, calm demeanor, too. G. was all about money. I could also tell that he'd do anything to anyone who tried to tamper with his operation.

We never knew their real names, so we did the same thing–gave people our street names. In fact, we didn't want to know their real names and they didn't want to know ours, either.

By this time, Val and her mother helped me secure my first apartment. It was on the West Side in a place called South Park, but all of my dealings were on the East Side. The main function of my apartment was to give me a place to lay low if anything went down. My crew were the only ones who knew where I lived.

The Detroit Boys, however, would lease a single home

under someone's name–usually a female one of them may have dated. They didn't like duplexes because they wanted to keep a low profile. They were very strategic and selective in the whereabouts of their locations. My crew and I managed the locations for them, because the Detroit Boys barely spent time in those spots. For the most part, they'd refill our supply of crack, give us some money, and then they'd split. And we never asked any questions.

When I look back, though, I see that we hardly made any money with them. They just kept us drunk and high. We had fifths of Tanqueray, Hennessy, Alizé, Jack Daniels, Moët and more. The Detroit Boys never smoked weed from Ohio, either, arguing that it wasn't nearly as good as the pounds they brought from Detroit.

When we were hungry, we'd send a dope fiend to the store for us. They sold us books of food stamps for little to nothing. We could get fifty dollars worth of food for three dollars worth of crack, if not less (depending on how desperate the person was). By the end of our time working with the Detroit Boys, we ended up with four locations.

We called our main location "The Mother Layer" because it was the most profitable and consistent spot. All of the windows had bars on them. Each entrance was barricaded to slow down any intruders, robbers, enemies and especially the police. We placed a battery-operated doorbell on the back door, and we kept the actual bell in the room where we were situated. We never set up in the kitchens because that's where we did all of our sales. No one was ever allowed to go past the kitchen. It was a drug dealer's bootcamp. Because we never sold drugs outside of any of our spots, we were able to keep a low profile. We tried not to bring any unwanted attention our way.

We knew most of the other drug dealers on the East Side, but what they didn't know is that we were the ones who had been taking all of their customers. We learned how to cook crack, and we learned how to chop it up and divide it. Chopping up crack took skills and creativity. We had to be able to use a razor blade to cut up the blocks, and the blocks never came in a perfect square. Once they were broken up, we learned how to count them out. We also knew how much money to expect from each block.

An eight ball was about three to three-and-a-half grams, which cost a hundred and twenty-five dollars back in the 90s. By the time it was broken down into pieces, we ended up with around three hundred dollars worth. Revenue was determined by location of the sale, desperation of the client, and potency of the crack.

The Detroit Boys taught us all of their methods. The dope was cut up into twenty dollar pieces, and we sectioned them into groups of five. We put the sections on a large plate along with any crumbs, and we sold everything down to the last crumb.

We always had guns, too, from 9mms, to .45s, to S-Ks, to AK-47s, along with a host of other guns. Nobody ever answered the door alone, either. Only the police ever came to the front door. If we didn't know them, we didn't sell to them. Anyone who came into the spot would get a pat-down anyway.

We sold drugs in the spot week after week without leaving, and even on our worst days, we made thousands of dollars. On a good day, we made over five grand, easy. People spent their money in chunks: twenty dollars here and fifty dollars there. By the fifth of the month they were flat broke and didn't have any money left to pay their bills. Throughout the rest of the month, they did anything and everything to supply their addiction until the next month came. They stole clothes and TVs for us. They sold us their children's video game systems, food stamps and household products. If they had a car, we rented it from them for hours and we gave it back when we felt like it. But one of the saddest things, outside of seeing parents sell their children's things, was seeing women sell their bodies just for a small hit.

We had all been away from our families for a long time, and they didn't know where to find us. Those close to us were worried. Val was very worried and concerned about our relationship. She was getting tired of me leaving for long periods of time without telling her my whereabouts. Once I got into the spot, I cancelled all communication with the outside world. After a while, though, the guys decided that things were going well enough that each of us could take a break. We could do it if we took breaks in shifts. The guys even insisted that I went first, because deep down inside they knew that I really shouldn't have been selling drugs. I knew I had some making up to do, especially with my daughter.

The night before my break, one of our clients came in crying. In fact, she was a runner, whose primary job was to inform their associates of our product. G. and Smoke would scout the new areas for the most aggressive fiends. They'd give them samples of our product and promised them something free as payment for each person they brought us. The runners were the only ones allowed to purchase directly from us. If their associates wanted our product, they had to go through our runners.

The runner was crying and told us one of the local drug dealers threatened to kill her if she continued buying drugs from us. We did all we could do to protect our investment, assuring her that nothing was going to happen to her. After that, one of my partners decided to provide some scare tactics to one of the local drug dealers.

From the upstairs bathroom window, Ryan had been watching the alley for intruders. He warned us when he spotted a guy hiding down the alley behind a dumpster. I was still in the kitchen with our runner and one of my partners. After Ryan's warning, my partner traded me his .45 for my

9mm rifle, and then he headed out into the alley. I watched from the ground floor. Ryan covered him from the upstairs window. Once he got into the alley, my partner made some type of *Scarface* comment and then let off a gunshot before coming back inside the house. He was so quick, the neighbors never saw him.

We had to play things safe, so we immediately gathered all of our things– drugs, television, games and anything else that kept us busy. Then we moved upstairs to the master bedroom, which was located in the front of the house. We figured that we were in danger of a drive-by, or at least some type of retaliation.

A few hours later, Ryan and I were walking down the hallway and we heard some shots. Ryan even felt some pass by his head. Then, we noticed a bullet hole through the curtain in the bathroom. It was evidence that the bullet had been half an inch away from hitting Ryan in the head. At that point, we were on red alert, ready for anything.

We normally took naps in shifts, but that night no one slept. Still, the guys felt like they had the situation under control and they encouraged me to take my break. I went to see Val and my baby. Val was angry at me, letting me know that I needed to get my priorities straight. I heard everything she said to me, too. In my mind, that's exactly what I was doing–making money to take care of them.

I spent the entire day with them, and the next day

I drove back to the spot feeling good that I was able to straighten things out with Val. I couldn't believe my eyes as I approached the house. It looked like Swiss cheese. Bullet holes were everywhere. Petrified and furious, I went in the back, trying to get into the house. I had no idea what happened to my crew. *What do I do?* I knew I wasn't going to be able to get in the house, and I couldn't risk anyone from that neighborhood spotting me.

I jumped back into the car and sped down the alley. I went to every single one of our rendezvous spots. I spent hours searching for my crew, and finally I saw them walking down the street. What a relief! My crew was alive.

They jumped in the car right away and told me the locals came back and turned the alley into a warzone. Bullets flew in both directions, busting through the windows and walls. Everyone was scared but they had to shoot back. Then they ran out of ammo, and they had to cover themselves as bullets kept flying. Eventually, the gunfire ceased.

Just minutes after the shootout, the police arrived to the scene and surrounded the house. A helicopter hovered overhead. The police did all they could to break in, but they couldn't because we had all of the doors and windows barricaded for instances just like that. The barricades gave everyone time to flush the drugs down the toilet.

The crew told me that after forty-five minutes, the police finally got in. When the cops reached them, they were already laying down face first in order to avoid some police brutality. The police took them to the nearest precinct, did some further questioning, and released them. I wasn't sure exactly why or how they had gotten away with everything.

From that point, we all decided to lay low for a while. I went to my apartment and tried my best to be a regular guy. I wasn't trying to get into any more trouble. We could have been robbed, beaten or even killed. We barely escaped going to prison. God really came through for us on that one.

CLOSE CALL

"Thinking is the hardest work there is, which is
probably the reason why so few engage in it."
~Henry Ford

I had no interest in selling any more crack. I was living rent-free in the South Park apartments on the West Side. Living at my apartment allowed me to keep more of a low profile. Even the people I knew in South Park didn't know about the life I lived on the East Side. Ryan and the other guys stayed out east, and they gave me a monthly utility check. The only bill I paid with that check, though, was the bill for weed and drinks.

Val's cousin, Herm, was the only person who knew what was going on in South Park. If I needed to buy or sell weed, he knew where to get it. He also knew who the drug dealers were, and I soon learned that there were only a few guys making all of the money. Through Herm I met others, and before long, we ended up forming our own crew. Herm's people welcomed me in and treated me like family. We had some of the best cookouts in the summertime.

One guy named "Black" really became like my brother. He was from St. Louis, Missouri, but we came from similar backgrounds. He told me that I reminded him of his brother who had been murdered in St. Louis. I didn't take that lightly. Later, I learned he came to Columbus to lay low. He was looking for a fresh start and did not want to get involved in the street life.

It felt good to not sell crack for a while. I was in a better place in my life. I was going broke, but I was able to spend more time with Val. She stayed on the East Side in Trevitt Heights with her mother. She would catch cabs, get rides, or even catch the bus to visit me. And even though things were going better, I still needed a job.

Black and I did all we could do to get jobs. We searched far and wide and we just couldn't land any employment. It was our fault, though, because we couldn't pass a drug test. In fact, we tried our best to find jobs that didn't require a drug test or didn't have anything to do with fast food.

Through all of my interaction on the streets, I stayed in "basketball shape," playing in regular pick-up games. One day, one of the drug dealers in South Park made the biggest mistake he could make: he pulled out a wad of cash and counted out at least a thousand dollars. I looked at Black and he looked at me. Without saying a word, we both thought the same thing: *These guys are getting money like this out here?* Both Black and I had been laying low and we never posed any type of threat to anyone. We weren't troublemakers, either. We stayed in our lane and everyone else stayed in theirs. But when we saw that cash, Black and I agreed that those guys weren't going to be the only ones making money.

We decided to put our utility checks together and go from there. Even though we didn't sell crack in South Park, we were well aware of all of its happenings. We knew that the police let patrol off by 12:00 a.m. The security guards got off at 1:00 a.m. We had plenty of conversations with security guards and we understood their patterns. Their jobs were to patrol the area by walking through the place and riding around in their vehicles. They enforced the rules, making sure that anybody banned from South Park stayed out. Most of the time, we saw the security guards chasing somebody through the apartment complex.

So Black and I understood the system. On top of that, we were cool with most of the dope fiends. They always kept us up-to-date on who was who, and we didn't even have to ask. Since some of the main drug dealers weren't well-liked, we knew it wouldn't be a problem getting the dope fiends to commit to us. We quickly identified our runners, and we planned to continue on with our same appearance so we wouldn't raise any red flags. That enabled us to still walk the neighborhood freely without looking suspicious.

We both pitched in thirty-five dollars from our utility checks. From there, the rest was history. We did exactly what we set out to do. I made way more money than I did with the Detroit Boys, and I still continued to walk around the neighborhood freely. I used what the Detroit Boys taught me and I incorporated it out west. The guys in the hood knew me as Mike Dean, but my customers and associates knew me as "Money." By having my clients call me Money, it kept some of the other drug dealers and security guards guessing who "he" was.

One night Black came over to my house in distress. He said, "Mike, I have to go back to St. Louis!" He told me that the guy who killed his brother threatened his little sister.

"I'll go with you," I said. "Let me finish selling the rest of my dope and we can get on the road."

"Fine," he told me. But before I could finish selling what I had left, he jumped on the road without me. Black never returned to South Park after that.

I was a bit perturbed, but I stayed in South Park and the money kept coming and coming fast. I was making money hand over fist. The only time I sold drugs out in the open was from 3:00 a.m. to 6:00 a.m. After that, I went inside like Count Dracula before the sun came out. I hit the block hard, and I began jumping in and out of cars making sale after sale. At that hour, most of the other dealers were sleeping. During the weekend, they would be at the club flashing their money around, which was fine by me, because I was making money around the clock.

Soon, I started making too much money to not be noticed by the drug dealers. But by then I had staked my claim. We weren't friends; we didn't hang out. They didn't talk to me and I didn't talk to them. I was so engulfed in the street life that it started making me mean and my heart was growing black and frigid. I was all about money.

I kept Val and the baby out east, even though she would do her best to come to my house. I couldn't risk her getting hurt, and she would have slowed me down. I preferred her to stay out east, and that way I could go visit when I had time. I was safer out in Trevitt, anyway. I grew up with most of the people out there. As the money grew, however, I became more and more careless. I started getting prideful and puffed up, and I began to break my own rules.

Then, one of my cousins and I got into a debate. He was a fellow dealer and our discussion was foolish–all egotism. He thought he made more money where he sold drugs, and I was confident I was making more out west. The discussion all started because he didn't believe me when I told him I was making money out west. We came to the conclusion that we would go to each other's areas and let the evidence speak for itself.

We started at his spots. He made a lot of money but it wasn't fast enough. What he didn't know was that I had set up a system that enabled me to make money really fast, almost nonstop.

First of all, I cooked my own crack and I made sure that it was more potent than anyone else's. Prior to that, one of my suppliers was a guy who knew my big brother, Nard. He was giving me good deals, but my customers started complaining that the drugs they got from the East Side were a lot better. I didn't smoke crack or snort cocaine, so I had to rely on my runners to make sure I was serving the best product.

Then one of my suppliers sold me a batch so bad that I had to re-cook it. Doing that, however, gave me a great advantage. My runner told me if I kept my product like that, I would make a lot of money. The other dealers didn't have the quality of crack I had. With that, I was able to name my price. When I changed the quality of my product, I was able to make four times the amount on a normal rock. I also tried not to raise too many red flags with my suppliers, so I never bought large amounts from them. Instead, I bought small amounts daily from three different suppliers. That also helped me to not have large inventory on hand. The only problem was that even though I wasn't selling drugs from my apartment, my clients knew where I lived. South Park was located in a secluded area, and for the most part, it was a standalone housing project.

My cousin and I finally got to my neck of the woods. I couldn't wait to show him how I did my business. Truthfully, I had an ulterior motive. Dealing was becoming too much for me to do alone, and I needed someone to have my back. It was hard to find somebody I could trust. But one thing that drew me to this particular cousin was that he was all about making money.

Before he came, one of my runners went shopping for me. I wanted to show him how I was living in the hopes that he would come out to South Park with me. At my pad, drinks were everywhere, and we ate seasoned-to-taste T-bone steaks. We were having a blast, and right when I was ready to start pitching my sale, I heard someone knocking. I looked out the peephole and saw Val and the baby.

I did not want her to come out there. I did not like her coming to my house. I had too much going on and I didn't want to risk anything happening to them, so I asked her to go home.

"No," she said.

"I'll get you a taxi, and I will be at your mother's later on tonight," I coaxed. But she continued to refuse, so I gave in. Since she was there at the house, I had to stay in, too. All night, I was pacing the floor because I knew I was missing money. Clients paged me nonstop. I kept asking Val to go home, but she refused, so I let her stay.

How Did I Get Here?

Boom! Boom! Boom!

Customers pounded on my door left and right. Finally, I gave in to them, too. Every five minutes, I served them with whatever they wanted. My cousin and I made money hour after hour. The night grew late and everyone fell asleep, except for me. The money was coming so fast, I didn't have time to sleep.

As the night grew later and later, I started to get paranoid. Something was going to happen that night. I could feel it. My cousin and I had some beef with a guy who was ruthless, but that wasn't it. I had a feeling in my stomach. My family was still in the house sound asleep. I went in the bathroom and pulled out the large knives that I used to carry. One knife was like Rambo's and the other was a dagger. I was in the bathroom sitting on the toilet with the lid down. I began to glide the blades against each other, prepared for anything.

That's when I heard a knock. I kept all the lights in the house off, and then I walked to the door smooth and silent, like Bruce Lee. Through the peephole, I saw an unfamiliar dope fiend. I put one hand on my knife and the other on the knob, but something kept telling me not to open the door. I scanned the hallway and the coast was clear, so I opened the door.

"Who are you looking for?" I asked. The girl asked if I

had any dope. Something kept telling me to close the door. But I didn't. I didn't go back inside, either. Instead, I sold her the amount she asked for. After she left, I closed the door and looked out the peephole for about five minutes in case someone was attempting to rob me. I was on edge with my family in the house. Fully-submerged in frustration, I went back into the bathroom and resumed my position on the toilet with my knives.

BOOM! Someone kicked in the door.

I jumped off the toilet and headed toward the door, thinking it was a perpetrator. But it wasn't. It was SWAT. Someone yelled. Then I heard Val's voice: "My baby is in here!" I ran back into the bathroom and jumped in the bathtub. Before I could fully adjust myself, I got caught in the shower curtain and the next thing I knew, I had semi-automatic weapons and guns aimed at me and lights from everywhere blinded me. My body froze. I certainly wasn't trying to give anyone a reason to shoot me. Before they cuffed me, though, I got a good glance at one of the members of the SWAT team.

They dragged me out of the bathtub and that's when I noticed my cousin pinned against the floor. They didn't do anything to Val. She wasn't even cuffed. I was flooded with mixed emotions. On one hand, I knew the last person I sold to was up to something, but it was my fault for selling to someone I didn't know. I sold most of what I had except for a few small rocks–less than a hundred dollars worth. On the other hand, I was glad they didn't harm my family, especially my daughter. All I could do was look at my baby sound asleep and think to myself, *how did I get here?*

Once the SWAT team secured the premises, they traded us off to the Columbus Police. They looked like masked vigilantes, keeping their identities a secret. While being escorted out, I heard one of the neighbors cheering and yelling, "You drug dealer!"

I never *ever* thought I'd get caught.

WHAT'S HAPPENING TO ME?

I had never been in trouble before, and I didn't know what to expect. My only experience with jail was what I had seen on TV. I had no idea what was going to happen next. I was petrified. Before long, I'd gotten a mugshot and had been fingerprinted. They took the clothes I was wearing, bagged them up, and then stored them away. I had to fashion myself in the County Jail wear, and then I was escorted to the elevator and we made our way to the holding tank.

When I got to the holding tank, I looked around and said to myself, "This isn't too bad." There were bunk beds and I had a perfect view of the television just outside the window. I wouldn't call it "comfortable," but I admit that I was surprised. It didn't look as bad as I expected. It was a long night and I couldn't help thinking about Val and the baby. I couldn't wait to get released so I could go back and make more money.

Later, I heard keys jingling and unlocking the holding tank.

"Michael Dean, let's go!" yelled the guard.

I'm already in jail. Where could they be taking me?

We headed down the elevator and then I was stuffed in a van with several other guys. The van had bars on the windows, and the guards handcuffed me to a bar on the seat. I had nothing to say, so I kept quiet.

Eight minutes later, we arrived at Franklin County Correction Center, also known as the Work House. The name spoke for itself. That place had the worst smell I have ever smelled in my life. It was less than a mile from a waste plant. The guards were more alert, too, and they all had attitudes. I couldn't believe that they strip-searched me right out in the open.

Once they were done, I quickly put on my uniform. Included in this ensemble were some awful orange rubber sandals–used ones, too. There was no telling how many people wore them before I did. The building was freezing. The guards didn't reference people by their names, either. They called everyone "Prisoner."

How in the world do they think I'm going to stay warm with this? I thought, as I carried my small thin blanket down the glum hallway. I took everything in. This was a whole new world for me.

Each room contained about thirty to forty guys. The bunk beds didn't look comfortable at all, and they were all steel and they were bolted to the ground. I can only speculate what Val was going through in the meantime.

Still cuffed, I walked into cell tank "2 West 5." As soon as the door shut, I had to reach my hands through the hole in the door so the guards could take the cuffs off. Once I stationed myself in the next available bunk, I hit rock bottom like the WWE superstar Dwayne "The Rock" Johnson performing his finishing move on John Cena. Life had officially smacked me in the face.

I was exactly where I never wanted to be. What was I going to do? What was going to happen to me and Val? Was she going to leave me? Then I thought back to the SWAT raid. While I was cuffed, they sat me near Val for a minute. She leaned over and whispered in my ear: "Do you want me to hide the money? They aren't going to check me."

That was the moment that I knew she would be with me through thick and thin. And that was the moment I prayed a prayer from my heart and said to God, "If you get me out of here, I promise I will change."

I GOT YOU

"Trays up!" yelled the guard.

Everyone jumped out of bed and swarmed the door, grabbing their trays to eat breakfast. My hesitation told everyone that I was the new guy. The food looked like slop. Still, the guys made sure I grabbed my tray. I gave my entire breakfast away as they divided it among themselves.

Finally I had the chance to use the phone. I had to take a number and wait my turn. The first person I called was Val. She had been waiting nervously by the phone. She asked how I was doing, but I told her I didn't have much time to talk. I asked her to contact my "friends" on a three-way call to see if anyone could bail me out. But everyone she called said they didn't have the money to bail me out, even though I knew every single one of them had money.

While I still had some time left on the phone, I remembered Pastor Caldwell. I hadn't seen or talked to him for years. I knew that he'd helped people with problems similar to mine. I knew his number by heart, too, and Val dialed. I was nervous, hoping and praying that he would get me out. After the third ring, he answered.

"Hello, who is this?"

"This is…"

"Mike." He guessed it before I could even say my name. I briefed him on my happenings and then I asked him if he could help me.

"Have you called any of your friends?" he asked.

"Yes," I said.

He has to give me a yes or no, I thought. I was nervous, but I remembered that Ryan always said, "What's the worst a person can say?"

So once again, I prepared for a no, but expected a yes.

"All right," said Pastor Caldwell, "try and call your friends again, and if they won't help you, call me back."

I did exactly what he asked me to do, but my friends gave me the same response. So I called Pastor Caldwell back. He told me that he would be up there the next day to get me out.

At any point I knew I was going to be asked the most common question that inmates ask newbies: "What are you in here for?"

When someone finally asked me, the room instantly became silent. I stuck my chest out, and then spoke from my diaphragm to make my voice sound deep.

"Selling dope."

After they heard that, everyone went back to what they had been doing.

I noticed a guy watching me from the other side of the room. He asked me if he could talk to me, and he started asking me questions about my life.

"Man, I don't know you and you don't know me," he said. "But, you look like a bright guy. Will you do me a favor?"

"What's that?" I asked.

"Do something with your life," he said.

He was serious, too. I could tell we were about a year apart in age, and he told me that he had gotten twenty-five to life and he was about to be transferred to a prison in Alabama.

"You will only do about two weeks in here," he assured me. "But seriously, do something with your life."

"I got you," I promised him.

Pastor Caldwell was a man of his word. He paid my bail and I was out the next day. Right after the prison guard called my name, I heard another voice call my name.

"Hey, Mike." I looked back and it was the guy with twenty-five to life. "Don't forget what I said."

I nodded as I left.

I had some things to think about. I didn't want to fall victim and become a repeat offender. Although my money was confiscated by the police, making money wasn't going to be a problem for me. Clientele wasn't a problem for me, either.

I was free, and I didn't spend as much time in jail as I thought I would have. But, the moment I got to Val's, something came over me. All of a sudden, I had this crazy urge to go back to South Park and start up business. The streets were pulling me like the ring pulled Frodo Baggins in *The Lord of the Rings.* I wasn't strong enough to resist the temptation, so I yielded. I didn't have any money, but if I could borrow at least fifty dollars from someone, I knew I could get back in the game.

Going to any of my associates, however, was not an option. I had to find someone who I was "cool with," but someone I didn't "associate with." Then I remembered Big James, Val's sister's boyfriend. He and I had respect for one another but we never had any dealings until then. Val never had a clue.

Big James let me borrow the money. All this time, Val thought I was going to hang out with Ryan. Honestly, I felt like I was on my own without Ryan. He had decided to settle down with his girlfriend. He got a job and the two of them moved into a nice apartment in the suburbs. I couldn't risk getting him involved in the things I was in. In fact, I was a little mad at him, because I felt like he had left me. Not having Ryan with me made me even meaner. As much as I missed Ryan, though, I had deep respect for the decision he had made.

Nevertheless, I went back to my apartment like a dog after its own vomit. I located one of my most trusted runners and then I pulled an all-nighter. I made over five hundred dollars from the fifty dollars Big James loaned me.

The next day was a Saturday, and I was still in South Park, playing catch-up with some of the fellow drug dealers out there. We all decided to pitch in and get a bag of weed. Then, I saw a group of guys mowing the lawn. At first I didn't think anything of it until I noticed the man on the riding lawnmower. His face looked familiar. It was the SWAT guy.

I told my guys that the SWAT team was disguising itself as a lawn care company. They laughed it off, but I knew the system in South Park. Their workers were on duty only during the weekdays.

"Give me my money back. I'm out," I told them, and then I got out of there as soon as humanly possible.

That was the moment I snapped out of it. *I'm out. I'm done with the streets. It's time for a change. I must do something different or I'm going to be another statistic,* I thought. After that day, SWAT began busting all of the main dealers out there. As for me, I left and didn't look back. I knew that the whole reason I had gone to jail in the first place was because someone told on me. How else would they know to show up at my door? *If the game is like this and people have to snitch, I don't want to be a part of it any more,* I said to myself.

I figured that I would have at least a few encounters with law enforcement and other hustlers, which wasn't a problem. But I never took into account that a disgruntled person could just call the police one time and I would end up in jail. I knew that it was time for me to do something else with my life. In fact, most drug dealers I knew thought they would never get caught, either. But I saw some of the toughest dudes in my hood get caught slipping and either go to jail, or end up in a casket. Those same people who counted on making it big in the street life were reduced to nothing after the system put fines, probation, parole and future indictments on their lives.

I had nowhere else to go but back to the beginning with my mom.

I'm Tired of This

*"If you want to stay relevant, then you must
stay ahead of change."*
~Dr. David C. Forbes

Since my daughter had been born, reuniting with my mother wasn't as hard as I thought. Thankfully, I was able to stay with her until I figured out my next move. One way or another, the street life had to end for me. One day, Mom and I were standing on her front porch talking about the need for both of us to change our lives.

"Mikey, I'm tired of this," she said. "I'm so tired of the way I'm living my life, and if I don't start doing something different now, I may not get to see my grandbabies grow up."

Finally, after years of drug and alcohol abuse, she was ready to change. We both were. Tears streamed down her cheeks, and we both knew that looking back was a thing of the past. Change would require major sacrifices.

My mother checked into a drug recovery program called Amethyst. The Amethyst treatment program provided alcohol and drug treatment and housing for homeless women. Desperate for change, my mother gave up the life she was living. She stayed in the program for about two years, and was assigned to a small, two-bedroom apartment.

The biggest sacrifice she had to make was giving up one of her kids. For some reason, my brother Marv couldn't stay with her, so he turned to the streets. My mother's transition may have helped her, but it didn't pay dividends to Marv. He was caught up in his emotions, too. On one hand he totally celebrated our mother for her commitment to change. But on the other hand, he was left out in an elongated tunnel of darkness, mentally sentenced to a life of crime and violence.

Marv's peers became his main support group, and he qualified for their loyalty. They were all close friends with similar struggles. At the time, there wasn't anything my mother could do about Marv; she was too weak to help him. If she had stopped to help him it would have resulted in her own relapse, and she couldn't take that risk. In short, my mother was afraid of herself. On top of that, she was tortured with the fear that the child she had to leave behind wasn't safe. My mother knew that life all too well. All she could do was pray and ask God to help her child.

Marv understood that Mom had one chance to get better, and that chance was right then. He felt like he was mentally tough enough to withstand any challenge the streets could muster up for him. But even though he had the support of his peers, he was alone. Marv was sixteen, and his survival kit contained only a pack of rocks.

Marv soon found a new pack of wolves, and they had a "menace to society" mindset. Even so, they were good people behind all of the crime and violence. They never woke up one day dreaming of becoming drug dealers. They never put their hopes on serving twenty years in prison for being loyal and not snitching. They were people just like everyone else–people who idolized John Elway, Eddie Murphy, Barry Sanders, Michael Jordan, Charles Barkley and Deion Sanders. They mimicked their signature moves and the famous Heisman pose. When they played basketball, they let their tongue hang out like Air Jordan. They did the Ickey (Woods) shuffle, and just like Michael Irvin, they spiked the football to the ground when they scored a touchdown.

They were raised to be fearless and to trust no one. In fact, they were taught to impose their will on anyone who opposed them. We grew up in a life with parents who had their visions stripped from them through an imposed societal struggle. Going to school wasn't worth the time when they drove better cars than their teachers and principals.

Their role models, called "Old G's" (Original Gangsters), trained them how to rock cocaine into crack. They were engaged in criminal activity before they even got to middle school. By the time they were in their mid-teens, they were seasoned gangsters, not caring who stood in their way. They had a low tolerance for weaklings, and weak members of their crew soon found out that they were in the wrong group.

Before they hit puberty, they knew how to roll up marijuana. They smoked cigarettes. Some of them were drinking sips of gin before they could say their ABCs. It was the life they learned to love. My brother was comfortable with staying in that life while our mother was making changes for the better. Even though our mother had submitted herself to being better, Marv just wasn't ready to commit to such a life.

He was the first child out of my mother's children who went to prison, and her heart broke. Marv went to prison for felonious assault, and there was nothing my mother could do but to get her own life right. She was as supportive as she possibly could be while he was locked away.

Then Rodney got locked up for a similar crime and was sentenced to "juvenile life." He went in at the age of fourteen and was released at twenty-one. It was very hard for her to hold change true to form while her children were struggling in a life she once lived. Plus, she was fully aware of the traps that would lure her children. My mother was getting better, but her children were getting worse.

She fought hard not to sink into depression, but it caught

up with her. My whole family was hurt and stressed and full of grief. They didn't know how to cope with the pain of that life. It was only by the sheer grace of God that I made it out. Even though we had it hard growing up, our mother never intended for us to be criminals. She tried the best she could to give us curfews and to discipline us when we were disobedient. As time progressed and the addictions grew stronger, though, the parental guidance became obsolete. My brothers and my sister all became engulfed by the beast of the streets.

Thank God for Amethyst! The program had rules and a system in place that provided 24-hour support. They kept my mother busy with detox, counseling, relationship-building and a plethora of support services. Once she stepped into Amethyst, she couldn't look back even if she wanted to. She was in the residential part of the program for about a year. Upon completion of the residential component, she was still required to attend regularly scheduled meetings for the next ten years or so.

"The 12 Steps to Sobriety" was one of the greatest blessings that ever happened for us. I remember seeing my mother on her knees in the morning and in the evenings, thanking God. She never missed a day without getting on her knees and being grateful for her new life. And more importantly, she prayed for her children. Many people said my mother would never amount to anything, that she would die a drug addict. It was amazing to see her changed.

Her level of commitment to her new life was awesome. She was the most unselfish person I knew, and she quickly became a mentor to many while she received continued mentoring herself. She understood that no matter how bad things were for her, she knew that someone somewhere had it worse than she did.

One of the 12 Steps was for my mother to help other people after she had been helped. My mother's heart was moved toward people struggling in addiction. She invited people to dinner and gave them rides places. She encouraged them, and gave them money if it was needed. She was everything I ever wanted in a mom. She was wonderful! Our relationship bloomed to a level that can't be compared. Our love for each other reached the highest level of love: "agape" love, a Greek word for "unconditional love."

To see her walk in change was the gift of a lifetime. I didn't need another birthday card or even Christmas gifts for that matter, after witnessing how masterful God is in saving a lost soul.

YOUTHBUILD

My mother invited me to her meetings, but I never made time for it. I regretted not keeping her company, but my life quickly became consumed with opportunities. During this time, I moved in with Val at her mother's house. It was November of 1997 when Val saw an ad in the newspaper that said, "Earn while you learn: GED, construction training and job placement with potential earnings starting out at ten dollars an hour." She and I both agreed that it would be a good place for us. We signed up in the morning, and by the afternoon, Val and I both got callbacks. At the time, YouthBuild focused on construction training and was in partnership with Columbus Works, which focused on academics. But Val decided instead to go into nursing and become an STNA (State Tested Nursing Assistant). So she opted out of YouthBuild and I continued.

Finally, I had a chance to do something with my life. At the very beginning of my experience with YouthBuild, I was hesitant–a bit leery of change. But day after day, the program instructors chiseled away at my stonewall barrier. Changing was easier said than done. My change didn't come overnight, however. Even though I was finished with selling drugs, I didn't suddenly stop all my bad habits like smoking marijuana and drinking.

The opportunity was great, and the people there provided more than GED training and work readiness preparation. It was like a group of life coaches had joined forces with the goal of helping others in all aspects of their lives. The people who were there to help had a variety of backgrounds, too.

Mrs. Jacqueline Lewis Greer, a practicing attorney, taught a course on street laws. She knew what she was talking about, and she was able to consistently break everything down in a language that we all could understand.

Mr. Glenn Walter taught Anger Management, and I thought for sure he was a Jedi Master. He looked like he was a stockbroker on Wall Street, but the first thing he told us was, "I'm from Compton." I couldn't believe that a man who carried himself as professionally as he did was from the rough streets of Compton, California. He taught me how to deal with my anger, and I had some major anger issues, too. For quality services like that to be provided for us was nothing short of a blessing.

It was getting close to Christmas, and I wanted to be able to provide for Val and for my child without doing anything illegal to earn money. I landed a cleaning job in the evenings downtown at the Rhoads Office Tower located on Broad and High Street. YouthBuild made a commitment that if we made it through the first six weeks we'd earn a two hundred and fifty dollar bonus. So I went to YouthBuild in the mornings and to work in the evenings. I was able to make some honest money for a change, which also kept me out of trouble.

THE QUESTION

After school one day, I was at the bus stop on Broad and High heading home. Lots of people were getting off of work and some were just going to work. A lady dressed like a bag lady walked up to me. In fact, she looked just like the old lady at the subway station in the movie, *Coming to America*. She looked right at me and said, "Do you believe in God?"

"Who doesn't believe in God?" I responded quickly. She nodded her head and quietly walked away.

About five weeks later, I was at work and it was time for me to take my dinner break. I had a few bucks in my pocket, so I decided to go to the Wendy's on High Street. The fastest way and the most logical way for me to get there was through the alley. Suddenly, out of nowhere, the same homeless-looking lady walked up to me.

"Do you believe in God?" she asked. My eyes got big and honestly, I was a bit perturbed.

"You are the same lady who asked me that about a month ago," I said, stuttering my reply.

"I know. God is calling you in."

Nothing else was said, and we both took about five steps in opposite directions. But I was curious about her, so I cautiously did an about-face. The lady was gone. I never saw her again.

Once I completed six weeks with Columbus Works, it was time to build a house. Damond Porter, Al Cathy and Moses Don Moseley were our leaders and our construction staff. Damond nicknamed himself and the other two instructors "Me-Al-N-Mo." Other staff members were present, too, including Tony English, the director of YouthBuild.

I never thought I would love the program as much as I did, but YouthBuild didn't just train us; they discipled us. They looked us in the eyes each day and developed us into men and women. They taught us how to build a house. None of the participants started the program with any skills in construction. Sometimes they worked us like crazy in the winter and summer months, but I learned so much that once I left YouthBuild, I began my own career in construction.

They told me at the beginning that if I was focused throughout the program, I would earn my GED, get a job starting out at ten dollars per hour, and I could earn a scholarship from the AmeriCorps Education Award program once I completed over 900 hours of service in my community. More importantly, I gained a whole new "crew"–a family. Slowly, the people I used to hang with on the streets drifted away.

Later, they brought in John Dawson, a counselor from MaryHaven, and drug treatment services were offered. Week in and week out, he challenged us, but I wasn't going out without a fight. I was going to quit with the same motives I had when I started using in the first place: I would quit because I chose to and not because somebody chose it for me.

When John came to the jobsite to host a session, he had responses to everything that came out of our mouths. We tried to tell him that "weed was from the earth," but that didn't work for him. He didn't have to say much to show us how ignorant we were in regard to the effects of drugs and alcohol on our bodies.

He was so impressed with our work performance on the site, however, that he gave us our first side job without the supervision of our construction staff. We weren't actually sure how to estimate jobs at that point, but he paid us a very fair wage. After that, any time he needed work done on his house, he called me. Even if I wasn't sure if I could do the task he needed, he trusted me enough to figure things out on my own. I tried my best, and if I couldn't figure something out, I got advice and direction from someone.

Soon, more of the construction staff offered me opportunities to work on the side in the evenings or on weekends. I jumped at every opportunity because it helped bring in extra money. I knew how to hustle for money and was never afraid to work for it. I didn't want to miss any opportunity to earn money. After all, I was still a hustler by nature. I was just learning how to hustle a legitimate product.

Transformation didn't come overnight for me, though. It took time. But each and every day, I was making progress—one step at a time, one moment at a time. Before the program, I was on the verge of serving time in prison or even getting killed. I had no license, no vehicle, and no money. YouthBuild changed all that. When it was all said and done, Val and I secured our first apartment together in a quiet neighborhood. I made a commitment to Pastor Caldwell for helping me as a child, and then bailing me out of jail as an adult. I committed to go to church regularly. Then, upon completion of YouthBuild, I earned my GED, received an AmeriCorps Education Award, and got a job starting out at ten dollars per hour…just like they promised.

YOU DON'T BELONG HERE

I went to school for construction at one of the largest construction companies in Ohio. I got my driver's license and two vehicles: a 1991 Ford Taurus and a 1985 Ford Ranger. Tony sold me the truck for five hundred dollars, and I couldn't pass up that offer.

I volunteered every chance I could get. One day while I was doing work at Corna Kokosing, the owner had an all-employee meeting. He was initiating his plan to enhance the training and development of the apprentices. He said that every apprentice would have a mentor of their choosing. Mentors would help the apprentices develop their skills and they would also help the company develop more quality workers at the same time. By then, I'd been working with the company for over a year so I was pretty familiar with everyone there. We had a nice selection of journeymen to choose from, and I started to think of people who I thought would be a great fit for me as a mentor.

We worked on a big project in Delaware, Ohio called Methodist Theological School, about a forty-five minute drive away. I spent most of my time on that project when I worked for them, so I felt the best person to select as my mentor was our foreman, Kenny. He was the best of the best, and he seemed to be able to do anything. He was a specialist, too, and he didn't fool around with simple repetitious things. Instead, he was the guy who did all of the custom work. He'd still pitch in, though, when we needed extra manpower on simpler projects. Kenny had all of the latest tools in his two-pouch toolbelt. He led by example and he was very modest. When it was time to work, he worked hard. All of his completed tasks were done with his perfection written all over them. If I was going to choose anybody, he'd be my first draft pick.

Since all mentors were required to have their apprentices by their sides, I decided to ask Kenny to be my mentor one day while we were on the job. I waited until the snack truck pulled up to the site and honked its horn twice. Time for a break. Guys snacked on sandwiches and candy or they stood around and drank coffee. Some were laughing and joking, while others were frustrated because they were behind schedule. That was when I approached Kenny. I was excited, like it was my favorite holiday. I came at him as politely and humbly as I knew how.

"Hey, Kenny, I was thinking... I would be totally honored for you to be my mentor."

Kenny looked at me and took a sip of his drink.

"I can't do that for you," he said.

My joy and happiness deflated like a tire shot by a high powered rifle. He had to give me a reason. I wasn't going to let him get off that easy. I understood that if I wanted to be the best, then I had to learn from the best.

"Why?" I asked.

"Because you don't belong here," he said. Then he turned and walked away.

Out of all of the things YouthBuild taught us, they forgot something. They didn't teach me how to handle racism. When Kenny made that statement to me, I was knocked off-balance. As I looked around, I noticed that all the others who were just as qualified to be my mentor had walked off with him. I tried to remember what Mr. Walter taught me in class at Columbus Works about Anger Management. I thought about all of the life lessons "Me-Al-N-Moe" imparted to me. I thought I was doing a good thing by earning my GED and becoming drug and alcohol free. But for what? I couldn't change the color of my skin. I finally came to the realization that racism still existed in the minds of some. God must have known I was a changed man, though, because a year or so earlier I would have reacted much differently.

YouthBuild taught us that color didn't matter. They saw to it that we all felt a sense of love and respect. But it was obvious that not everyone operated according to YouthBuild's standards. Not too long after my exchange with Kenny, the company started shipping me around and cutting my hours back. Eventually, I was let go. I had to explain everything to Val, but she supported me and encouraged me to hang in there. I thank God for a companion like her who stuck with me through thick and thin.

In 2000, Tony offered me a position as a construction helper. I always wanted to work for the program. I took the position and worked to the best of my abilities. I was honored to become the second graduate on staff in the program's history.

Seize the Moment

One day, Gil Barno (YouthBuild's Executive Director) called me over so I could meet someone. Gil always got goosebumps when he saw young people's lives change through building affordable housing for low-income families. Young people who had never swung a hammer, used a saw, or even understood how to use a tape measure, all learned to work cohesively together. Gil was giving Terry Moran, a YouthBuild USA staff member, a tour of our jobsites. I shook Terry's hand, and I could see that he was the type of person whose mere presence made everyone smile.

Gil gave me a great introduction, too. Terry started telling me about YouthBuild USA's National Alumni Exchange. That year, it was going to be held in Orlando, Florida. He definitely had my attention. I knew this was my time to take life to the next level. Terry further explained the National Alumni Council (NAC). The NAC was peer-elected and members of the group were in charge of making key decisions for all of YouthBuild. NAC members also had important leadership roles at the national level. Terry talked about policy input, activism and advocacy. He told me that if I was interested, I would be able to run for a seat on the council. I was all in.

Terry then told me all the requirements and explained how to apply for the NAC. The principal, Dr. Joyce Swayne, helped me with my resume, speech and essay. She made my GED look like a Ph.D. Everyone in my program was rooting for me to succeed. There was no doubt in their minds that I would get a seat on YouthBuild's National Alumni Council.

While I attended the Exchange in Orlando, I met some of the most amazing and inspiring people I had ever met. Many of us had overcome similar struggles, but we all lived in different states. Graduates from all over the country were in one place operating on one accord. We celebrated and rejoiced in our successes and it was a great reinforcement to push us toward staying the course. Honestly, I had no idea that YouthBuild was so big.

It was time for the final component for a seat on the

NAC: the speech. I couldn't believe that after all I had been through and all I had seen, walking up front to deliver my speech made me so nervous. But I had come too far to give up. After I delivered my speech, I felt endorsed by the standing ovation, and it made me feel good about my chances. I then saw that they gave everyone after me a standing ovation as well. My heart began to race.

Ballots were passed out, and then collected. There were only a few positions, and I wasn't sure if I would make it. I had just met those people and some of the people who ran for the NAC already served on other committees for Youth-Build USA. Votes were tallied in another room, and finally the newly elected members of the National Alumni Council were announced. When my name was called I had such joy–winning the gold medal in the Olympics couldn't compete with how I felt.

Being a member of the National Alumni Council helped me to harness my leadership skills. I attended much training and built relationships with leaders from all over the nation. I took advantage of every opportunity I had. I wasn't just representing YouthBuild, I was representing my community, my family and other leaders who were coming behind me.

Once we left the NAC meetings or events, we had to go back to our realities. Even though we made changes that resulted in many successes, we all still had hills to climb. Many people weren't ready to make positive changes. Trying to motivate people back home was a constant struggle, but I tried to encourage them to do the right thing.

I Can Make It!

Ring! Ring! Ring! The phone rang at 2:30 a.m. I was sound asleep, ignoring the call. Ring! Ring! Ring! The phone kept ringing.

Who is calling me this early? I ignored the call again, but the phone rang again. I wiped the sleep out of my eyes and yawned as I stretched for my phone. I didn't normally receive calls at that hour. Someone on the other end was hollering and screaming, "Rodney has been shot! Rodney just got shot!"

"What?! Where is he? Which hospital?"

"He's not at the hospital… You just need to come downtown to Fourth and Chestnut."

I grabbed my keys and threw on whatever clothes were directly in my sight. I jumped in my car and drove. As soon as I got there, the first person I saw was my cousin, Nora. She was drenched in tears. In fact, everybody there was weeping. I saw yellow tape, and then I noticed that there wasn't an ambulance on the scene. The expression on my mother's face told me Rodney was already dead.

I dropped to my knees and began to weep with everything that was in me. Nobody could tame me. I remember balling my fists as tight as I could and squeezing them closed. I began pounding the ground with everything I had.

"NO!"

After about ten minutes of weeping, I was helped by some family. Tears still streamed down my face, nonstop.

"Where is he?" I asked.

They led the way. We had to walk through the alley and up the street, because the street that he was on was blocked off. Right before we reached the scene of the crime, Nora said to me, "Are you sure you want to remember him like this?"

"Yes," I said, without any regard for what I would see. I felt like I was in some type of dream world. Things weren't making any sense. Everything was moving so fast, too fast. Was I really ready to see him? Did I really want to see what I didn't want to see?

So Much Pain

Scattered around the yellow tape, turmoil was at its peak. The air was thick with pain...

HOW?!

How could this happen to my little brother? No. No. No! This can't be real! Lord, wake me up out of this nightmare! What did they do to my brother?! Who did this?! Why?! I can't take it! The hurt is eating me inside out. My mother is having a nervous breakdown, my family is crying everywhere. This can't be real. The news broadcasts reports of homicides all the time. But this doesn't happen to us! My brother Rodney is gone! Do I really want to see him like this? Do I really want to see my brother dead? This isn't Hollywood... This is the real thing. My thoughts were running a mile a minute.

Finally, we reached the scene of the crime. I saw him lying lifeless in the middle of the street. He was just lying there without his soul. The police officer on the scene handled him like he was a piece of meat at a butcher. Those cops didn't care about him, at least that's the way they made it seem. It wasn't like watching CSI where the detective looked concerned, trying to solve a homicide. Instead, the cops were smiling, laughing and joking. It was not the time for them to be laughing and joking. I was irate, as were my other friends and family members who were surrounding the scene.

Rodney's death sent shock waves throughout my family. I had to know what happened to my brother, and I investigated the best that I could. There were still so many loose ends, and we never learned the real truth.

Rodney had been released just before Christmas in 2003, after serving three-and-a-half years in Marion Juvenile Detention Center. As soon as he was released, his old buddies migrated like flies on manure to my mother's house. My mother did not approve of his friends because they all used to get in trouble together before he got locked up. The only thing that helped ease my mother's concern was that he was on probation. Rodney had to wear an ankle monitor strapped to his leg. If he went out of range or took the monitor off, his probation officer would be alerted. Noncompliance could have resulted in him returning to jail.

Rodney always asked my mom if he could go with his boys, and my mother's response was always no. That kept them away for a while. They tried again here and there, but she just didn't trust them. My mother had been Rodney's main supporter. She even got another job just so she could care for him and Marv while they were both locked up. The car she was driving was on its last leg, so she took a loan out so she could travel back and forth to visit my brothers. She did everything she could to support them while they were incarcerated.

Rodney bragged and boasted about how much he had improved in basketball during his years in Marion. Since I was going to play ball that day, I asked my mother if Rodney could hang out with me for a few hours to play some basketball. We played and we had an awesome time. A few days later, Rodney's friends asked my mom the same thing and she told them yes. But they never went to play ball. Instead, they went to the Short North. I got to my mom's that evening and she was fuming, pacing the floor.

"I'm going to find him," she said.

"I'm going too, and I will drive. Just tell me where to go."

"Go to the Short North," said my mother. She was a nervous wreck, determined to find her son. I drove until she told me to stop and let her out.

"Stay here," she said. "I'll be right back."

I saw her walk into the shadows of the night as she approached the apartment building about a stone's throw away. I sat in my car, blasting my music with JD's girlfriend in the back seat. Suddenly I looked up, and from a distance, I saw my mother arguing with someone. Once I got out of the car and moved toward them, I noticed the voice was Rodney's. He spoke freely, completely disrespecting my mother. It was completely out of hand. I jumped to try to intervene.

But he didn't care.

"I'm a grown man. I can do what I want to do, when I want to do it," he said. Things escalated and before long, I was at the point where I was ready to swing on him. The energy reverted from him and my mother to him and me. My mother attempted to calm us down. She even made him get in the car. When he got in, he slammed my door as hard as he could, and right when I was about to reach over the seat and hit him, my mother said, "Mikey, no!" She looked at me with the most distraught look I've ever seen. I listened to her and we went back to the house.

Later that same night, Rodney and a few of his friends

apparently went to the Flame, a weekend club for young adults. That's where things went sour. The next thing I knew, someone was calling to tell me he had been shot.

After the death of Rodney, my mother was consumed with hurt and confusion. I spent as much time as I could with her after that. She couldn't talk for weeks. One day my mother and I were standing on her porch, and she was so stressed, she picked up a cigarette and lit it. I took it right out of her mouth and then I hugged her tight for a long time.

It seemed like my mother blamed herself for Rodney's death. In her mind, he would still be alive if she had not gotten involved in the street life. She never recuperated after that. When I look back at our life before the crack epidemic, my mother could have had a productive life. But the epidemic caused shockwave aftermaths. The death of Rodney was an aftermath. Marv's incarceration was an aftermath. My life in the streets was an aftermath. And while my mother was blaming herself for her lack of parenting, she didn't take into account the outside influences. Those outside influences greatly contributed to the success and derailment of the community. I heard that it takes a village to raise a child.

That's what makes the Hood a Neighborhood.

HERE WE GO AGAIN

"Lord, if something happens and another one of my family members gets shot, please let him stay alive long enough for me to get to the hospital to pray for him." That was my prayer after Rodney died.

Exactly four weeks after the death of Rodney, I got a call. My older brother Nard had been shot four times and he was in critical condition. But he was alive! I got to the hospital as quickly as I could.

"I came to pray for you," I told him. Even though he was hooked up to an IV and machines kept him alive, we were very blessed to not have to bury another brother.

"It's time to change," I told Nard.

Just when I thought change was secure in my life, the challenges of life did not cease. I was very fortunate to have good people to support me through my time of grief and pain, though. Staff and students at work, members from the church, and people from the NAC and YBUSA were all there to support me. Support was great, but support itself didn't take the pain away. I did my absolute best to comfort my mother.

"We are going to make it through this," I told her. When I had the chance to be by myself, though, I'd break down and weep. I just couldn't understand why all of this was happening to us.

Continuing my quest for better days, I finally understood that in order to stay changed, I had to keep moving forward.

THE MAN I NEVER KNEW

"Be the change you wish to see."
~ Gandhi

When I was a young boy, my mother started unveiling pieces of my puzzle. Once, she sat me down and made me aware that I had sisters. I was more inquisitive than Curious George, but all she knew was that my sisters and I were in the same age group. She wasn't exactly sure how many sisters I had, but she thought I might have had three.

Periodically, my mother would take me to my grandmother's house–my father's mother. Her expression always said, "Sandy, why did you bring this boy over here? And you know he's not my grandson." She always made me feel unwanted. I probably saw her about five to eight times in my whole life. Most of the time, it would be in passing. It always seemed like my mother knew that she knew I was her grandson, but she never admitted it.

Unfortunately, my grandmother passed away and we really never had a chance to get to know each other. I didn't know anything about her. I didn't know how old she was, and I didn't know her favorite color. I didn't know how her cooking tasted. I didn't know which secret recipes had been passed down through the years. If only she would have given me a chance. I would have been one of her favorites for sure.

It got to the point that whenever my mother wanted to take me to visit my grandmother, I became reluctant to go. Still, how I was treated as a child didn't stop me from my quest to meet my other siblings. By the year 2000, I was determined to meet them. Enough was enough.

It was New Year's Eve, and I was bringing in the New Year at a church. As the clock got closer to midnight, the pastor instructed the congregation to begin the New Year with prayer and ask God for whatever we wanted. He quoted Matthew 7:7: *"Ask, and it shall be given to you; seek, and ye shall find; knock, and it shall be opened unto you."*

His last statement was to leave our request in the hands of God. He told us not to worry and he assured us that our requests would come to pass.

What do I want?

It wasn't like asking a genie for a wish. This was a prayer, and I took prayer very seriously. I had lots of things I needed in my life: a nice raise, a better car, a nicer place to stay. But what I really wanted most was the chance to meet my sisters.

My prayer was simple: *I want to meet my siblings.* That's it. Nothing else. I had never seen them. In fact, I didn't care what they looked like. I didn't care if they were rich or poor. I didn't care about their social status. I didn't care if they were blind, crippled, or even crazy. None of that affected my desire to meet them. After that brief prayer, I felt relieved from my strong desire and my informal quest of uniting with them.

About three months later on a Friday, I was having car trouble and I called a friend of mine named Big Kurt. He was one of the most reliable mechanics and friends I ever had. In fact, I considered him to be more of a big brother and mentor than just a friend. When I told him what was going on with my vehicle, he said, "I'll take a look at it when I get off work." He ended up getting off a little later than he expected, but he stopped by anyway. The day was drawing too dim for him to give me an accurate assessment, though, and he wasn't prepared to work in the dark. He said, "Let's wait until tomorrow and I will fix either your Explorer or your Ranger."

Kurt was getting ready to head home, but I asked him if he wouldn't mind taking me to grab a bite to eat first. He graciously said yes. The two of us ended up getting a Donato's Pizza and watching *The Matrix* back at his place. We had a blast together. In fact, that was my first time watching *The Matrix*, and the movie blew my mind. Just before we pulled away to go back to my place, Kurt's phone rang. Of all people, it was Dee calling him. Kurt told Dee he would hook up with him after he "dropped Mike off."

"Mike who?" Dee asked over the phone.

"Mike Dean," Kurt said. Immediately, Dee asked if he could speak to me. Dee and I had grown up together and we were like brothers, but we weren't the type of brothers who always got along. Still, neither of us was the kind to hold grudges, at least not for long.

Dee and I talked some small talk and then he told me that he had met one of my sisters.

"Who, Fee?" I asked.

"No, not Fee," he said. "One of your sisters on your dad's side. She wants to meet you."

Meet me? My heart was overjoyed with an unexplainable excitement. All I knew at the time was that I wanted to meet my sisters; for them to want to meet me was the cherry on top.

"Give me the number!" I said with excitement.

Kurt couldn't drive fast enough, and the fact that he kept driving the speed limit really frustrated me. My mind was racing like I was in the Indy 500. While he was driving, I called the number. The phone picked up after the first ring.

"Hello…"

Suddenly, I didn't know what to say. I had waited for that moment for so long, and there it was. But I froze. I wasn't sure how I would be received. Before I knew it, though, I had directions to her house and she was expecting me. I hung up and looked toward Heaven.

"Thank You. Thank You." I repeated it over and over: "Thank You." My prayers had been answered.

When Kurt pulled up to my house, I jumped out before the car could fully park. I couldn't wait; they were waiting for me. I rushed in the house, woke up my mother, and gave her a brief summary of what had transpired. She managed to give me a tired smile. That smile said to my heart, "Good things happen when your heart is pure."

I borrowed my mother's car. I was full of excitement and anticipation. That night, I didn't need a GPS to remember the directions I was given over the phone.

Finally, I pulled up to the house. It was the middle of the night and the house was dark except for one light shining from a downstairs window. The old wooden porch stairs squeaked with each step under the weight of my body. I took one more deep breath before I knocked on the door.

I heard footsteps coming closer, and the door slowly opened. I had asked God and He made it happen. I knocked and the door opened. After being invited to come in, I was greeted with hugs from everyone. Smiles and wonder painted their faces. I imagine they were asking the same kinds of questions inside themselves that I wrestled with for years. The rest of that night we tried our best to play catch up, but one night couldn't make up for years of lost time. Questions were coming from every direction.

That night made me the happiest man in the world. On my way out, I jumped in the air and clicked my feet together like a child. From then on, I visited them every day. I constantly gave God thanks for answering my prayer.

During that time, I met another sister and her son, and I repeated the reunification process with her, too. She and I were only about two weeks apart in age. I wanted so badly to be in their lives and I wasn't expecting anything from them but acceptance.

I was already accepted by so many others. I was becoming a minister. I was traveling the U.S. with YouthBuild, enhancing my life skills. I'd started my own small construction company. I'd pick up small odd jobs to continue to build my reputation. I was playing the drums in a local community choir. Val had given birth to our second child, and my family had become a sanctuary of love and acceptance. On top of every good thing, connecting with my siblings was nothing short of a blessing.

One day, I stopped at my sister's home. As soon as my nieces and I laid eyes on each other, we rolled around on the floor, laughing and having a merry time with each other. But my sister had a funny look on her face. I could tell she had something to say to me. I caught my breath and shifted my focus from my niece, who was still trying to play.

Suddenly, my sister said, "You know, you might not be my brother. You need to go around people who already love you."

I was stunned. It was like I had been slammed to the ground by speechlessness and handcuffed with astonishment. What could I do? How does a person respond to that? I released my niece and got up from the floor. Then I picked up my things, took one last look at my sister and my niece, and then I left.

I really thought that everything was going to go perfectly once I reconnected with my siblings. I imagined our children growing up together, and all of us spending holidays together. My niece was only nine years old, and in the blink of an eye, she would be grown. I didn't want to miss making memories with them, but there was nothing I could do.

My sister's statement was harsh, but at the same time, I understood. If I wasn't her brother, then I was just a stranger. The situation was just as new for her as it was for me. She probably didn't know what to think, either. From what I gathered through the years, she and our dad had a close relationship. During that time period he was in jail, waiting to finish his trial. Perhaps the news got back to him. Maybe he told her that I wasn't his son, and that everything I said was a big mistake. If so, her allegiance to him had to be loyal. Still, the most hurtful part wasn't so much my sister's comment as much as it was the realization that I would have to watch my niece grow up from a distance.

On the other hand, one of my other sisters and I became like two peas in a pod. She truly was a godsend. What I wanted to accomplish with my other siblings, I was able to do with her. We spent hours upon hours getting to know each other. We even created nicknames for each other. The connection we had was unexplainable. She became a part of my inner circle of support. Even though we didn't have the luxury of being in each other's lives through our adolescent years, we are taking advantage of the life that we have left on this planet.

The Man I Never Knew

Periodically my mother and sister suggested that I visit my father while he was in the county jail during the time of his trial. Their badgering really got on my nerves. As much as I had wondered about my father and imagined how life would have been different with him in it, I didn't want to make an effort to see the person who had abandoned me all of my life. I felt like I didn't need him. He should have been there for me and he wasn't–by choice. I didn't hate him, but I didn't care for him. How can you care for a man who was never there? Why should I have made any effort to find him when he knew exactly where I was? Shouldn't he have been trying to find me?

Why should I pursue someone who didn't care if I lived or died? And what if I had died as a victim of the streets? Would he have come to my funeral?

My mother and sister already knew what he looked like. If they saw him at a gas station or supermarket, they'd recognize him. I wouldn't have known him if he and I were at Subway in the same line together ordering a meal. At that point, we had never even had one conversation with each other. Why start then?

Maybe that's how my one sister felt about me. Maybe that's why she didn't receive me into her life.

All of those years went by and he had plenty of chances to connect with me. After a while, I officially closed the doors of my heart toward wanting that kind of relationship with him. But I never stopped wondering what my life would have been like with him. His lack of action, however, had spoken louder than his lack of words. Still, my mother and sister pushed me to see him.

When I didn't see my father at the park that day, that was it for me. I knew I was going to have to go through life without my dad. I wasn't vengeful; I just came to grips with my reality. Over time, I had worked to free myself from the pressure of feeling like I had done something wrong. I had come to grips with the truth that I might never know my dad. I didn't leave him, he had left me. His absence was his choice, not mine.

What if I went to visit him and he wasn't there again, like when I was thirteen? It was exhausting to search for a man who was never there. What if he didn't even care that I was there? What if he didn't speak to me? What did he look like? Did I look like him? My thoughts piqued my curiosity. What did he sound like? I wondered if I was taller than he was. But I was afraid of the risk of being hurt again.

"I'm a man, now," I told my mother. "I don't need him, and he doesn't need me. I'M A MAN!"

I tried my best to act like I didn't care. But deep down inside, I knew I had another opportunity to "go to the park" again. All of my close friends said I should go for it. They said that opportunities like that are often once in a lifetime. So I asked my sister to give me the information I needed so I could go down to the county jail to visit him. She gladly gave me all of the information. I finally decided to get it over with. That way, I would get them off of my back and let life happen.

The official at the county jail asked who I was visiting and they requested my ID. Then she asked me some questions.

"What is your relationship to the inmate?"

I paused. That was the toughest question I had ever been asked in my life.

"Sir… Your relationship to the inmate?"

My heart was pounding. My palms were sweaty. I never had the need to respond to such a question before.

"S-s-s-o-n," I stuttered. I watched her write the word on her paper. A guard then instructed me to get on the elevator and go to a certain floor. Once I arrived, then I had to wait by one of the windows until he came out.

The elevator took me right to the visitation floor. Each visiting booth was made up of two-foot wide glass, which was at least an inch-and-a-half thick and was cased in heavy-gauge metal. It was so thick that just talking to the glass didn't make sense. It was practically soundproof, unless all the visitors yelled at each other. Instead, each booth was equipped with an old-style phone booth receiver. I didn't know where to go, so I watched other visitors randomly find their booths. Since I didn't know what he looked like, I didn't even know who to look for. Inside, my emotions were flying everywhere.

The guys began coming out one at a time. They walked to their visitor booths and they began greeting each other. Soon, I was the only one left still standing by the elevator. Finally, I saw him. I saw him before he saw me. He stationed himself at a booth and he began to look around to see who came to visit. He certainly wasn't expecting me.

I walked over to the window. All I could do was stare at him, not knowing how to initiate the conversation. Eyeball to eyeball, he looked at me and I looked at him. We each picked up our phone receivers.

"Who are you?" he asked. I kept my head up, stuck my chest out, and looked him right in his pupils. I deepened my voice, too.

"I'm Sandy's son," I said.

"Oh." He paused and pondered for another moment. "I knew this would happen one day."

My dad was very calm, which made him hard to read. His demeanor was laid back. Once I told him who I was, he was systematically cautious with his words.

Conversing with him was like being in a chess match with my older self. After he made his first statement, I thought, *good move*. I don't believe he was trying to be insulting. In fact, it was a great way to begin. He put me in check by trapping me in a corner with his queen and pawn. His trap was temporary, though. I repositioned myself with a comeback move: "I'm Sandy's son." My answer captured his attention. His look of wonder signaled a flashback about his experience with my mother.

I didn't need to tell him my name. He knew who my mother was. It was written all over his face. In addition, I wanted to let him know that she had raised me without his assistance. I wanted to show him that I was alive and kicking. But his response, "I knew this would happen one day," put us both at a stalemate. After that move, our conversation was basically over. There was nothing more to say that would have added any substance. He tried to control the conversation after that, but I wouldn't let him.

He really didn't have much more to say, so I left it right there. I don't think I even used all of my visitation time. The visit didn't bring me any closure and I still wasn't affirmed. Additionally, I wasn't planning on coming back to see him any time soon. I don't think he would have cared, anyway. I wrote him a letter afterward, expressing exactly how I felt. Since then I haven't seen, or even heard from him. That was in 2004.

Not You—Not Now

It was December of 2006, and I was visiting my mother, as I often did. She was still in bed when I got there. She had been suffering from migraine headaches. I sat down on the edge of her bed. She smiled.

"I love you, Mikey," she said.

"I love you, too, Mom."

"Mikey… Do you forgive me?"

"Mom, you don't have to ask me that. I'm proud of you. As a mother, you are perfect to me."

And it was true. I was so proud of her. She was finally free from drugs and alcohol, and she had started her own small cleaning company. She became the most loving grandmother on earth. Truly, she adored her grandbabies. I think she tried through her grandkids to make up for what she was unable to do for her own kids.

My mother took my hand. "I'm not worried about you, Mikey. You take care of my grandbabies and your brothers and sister, okay?"

"I will, Mom."

"And don't leave YouthBuild. It's going to take you far."

"Yes, ma'am." I smiled at her. She smiled, too.

Once our conversation was over, I hugged her and told her I loved her. Then I kissed her gently on her forehead. She seemed to be doing well, except for those migraines. In fact, she was becoming a very healthy eater. She even went to the gym daily using her membership at Victory Fitness.

Then, about a week later, I got a call at work from a representative from Riverside Hospital. The lady was very calm and polite, explaining that she got my phone number from my mother's phone.

"How can I help you?" I asked.

"Sandy's doctor would like to speak to you," she said with a gentle voice.

"Why?"

"I think you need to come in."

My mother had been in the hospital several times, and she always wanted to keep a low profile, so I never told people when my mother was sick. I did tell the guys on the job-site that I had to run to the hospital and that I would be back shortly. The representative from the hospital didn't talk to me like the situation was an emergency, so I made it there without any sense of urgency. I was escorted to a small, private room, and I was told that the doctor was on his way to talk to me about my mother's condition.

"What's going on?" I asked her again.

"The doctor will give you all of the information you need," she said.

The lady was really nice, so I relaxed and waited to see the doctor. I wondered what was going on with my mom.

The doctor had a small group of people with him when he came in the room. He calmly started to explain the events that took place with my mother.

"Your mother was in a car accident, but the accident itself wasn't bad…"

She still must be unconscious or just resting, I thought. *Perhaps they wanted her to rest until they let people visit her. Perhaps her condition wasn't stable enough.*

"Can I go see her?" I asked.

Then the doctor's demeanor changed. He told me she was rushed to the hospital, and then he rattled off a long list of procedures they went through upon her arrival.

"We did all we could do," he said gently.

"What?!" I shouted. "What do you mean you did all

you could do?!"

"By the time we got her, she was already gone. I'm sorry."

I ran down the hospital hallway, blinded by the nonstop tears in my eyes. I busted through the rotating doors at full speed. I didn't know where to go. I couldn't catch my breath. My heart pounded.

I was still running.

I couldn't see.

My face was covered in sweat and tears. My nose drained all over my face, and I didn't even care. My heart and soul were ripped and fragmented, bursting in every direction. I tripped and fell and I still didn't care. I nestled myself in the field by the main entrance and wept. I wept for at least an hour before I could even call anyone.

Not long afterward, Aunt Phil was found dead. Two years later, Big Marv died. Fortunately by then, my relationship with him had reached a better place, and I knew that he had developed a kind of love for me. He wasn't much support while I was growing up, but perhaps he didn't quite know how to love or support me–another man's son. Perhaps he knew how I was conceived and it was too hard for him.

Then, Pastor Caldwell passed away. He had been one of the most influential people in my life.

This is hard for me to say, but the dad I never had was all I had left. So, if he someday decided he wanted a relationship with me, I would be all in. When and if the opportunity presented itself, I would forgive and go from there.

I don't fully understand the relationship that transpired between him and my mother at my conception. I'm sure every child would like to believe that he or she was conceived out of some type of love. Perhaps in time, my dad will face his inner demons. Perhaps he will find it in his heart to at least get to know his great contribution to this world: me.

WHAT IF I HAD A FATHER?

"We need fathers to realize that responsibility does not end at conception. We need them to realize that what makes you a man is not the ability to have a child–it's the courage to raise one."
~ *President Barack Obama*

The lack of affirmation from my father trickles down to my children. Unfortunately, it doesn't stop there. It trickles even further to their children and their children's children.

If you don't do it for this generation, think about the next generation. Think about your grandbabies who may never sit in your lap or call you "Paw Paw" while you share with them all of the wisdom you gained through your life experiences. Think about missing out on pushing them on the swing set, seeing them laughing and smiling saying, "Push me higher, Paw Paw. Push me higher!" Think about the holidays and birthdays you may never share. Think about all of the things you have missed along with all of the things that you will miss.

Childless father, you are on the verge of missing out on moments that you cannot get back. You must figure out how to re-engage yourself back into your rightful place. You don't have to have a lot of money. You don't have to have a big house or drive a fancy car. You don't have to be Muslim, Catholic, Jewish, or even a Christian to be a father. Father-lessness affects more than meets the eye. This generation is hoping with all of its might that you'll find it within your heart to come back. It's not going to be easy, but it's worth the ridicule. It's worth the embarrassment. It's worth the shame. It's worth the heartache. You can do it! We believe in you! Just try! At least make a move. Push past all the chatter. Push past the inner turmoil that has your soul trapped. Your children need you more than you may ever know. We are in this together! Trust and believe it's going to be painful at the beginning, but have faith and things will work themselves out.

PROGRESS THROUGH THE PROCESS

With the sudden back-to-back deaths that happened in my family, a lot of the responsibility of handling those outcomes landed on me. As the oldest, and seemingly the head of two families, I dealt with my grief when I had time. It was necessary for school to take a back seat while I ensured the well-being of my family stayed intact. Staying focused wasn't an easy task for me, and I had to drop out of college.

Even though I haven't yet finished my degree in business, I never quit my pursuit for greatness. My mother always told me that I was a great man and that my level of influence would increase, putting me in a better position to help others.

After my brother Rodney died, and about a month after my older brother Nard was shot, my cup was empty. I was finally at a point in my life where I really didn't mind giving up.

Stress was trying to chain me and depression was slowly seeping in. Sometimes, I broke down while out in public with some of my friends. Whether it was at the main entrance of a bowling alley, or some restaurant, the tears just came out of nowhere. I was hurt! And I had very few people in my life who could fully understand my pain.

At that time, Bishop Noel Jones happened to be in town, ministering. Outside of TD Jakes, Bishop Noel Jones was second to none. It seemed like I had every ministry product (tapes and CDs) he put out. During all of the mayhem my family endured, I had nowhere else to turn but to God.

The Higher Ground Church was jam-packed and no empty seats could be found. I had to squeeze in between people who barely had room to sit themselves. I was in a man-sized sardine can. Nevertheless, I was expecting something that night that would be uplifting and would give me the space to release as much of my pain to God as possible.

During those times, I did all I could do to cope with the pain that muzzled my soul. Even while being around people, I still felt like I was by myself. The only thing I knew to do, just like when I was a kid, was go to church. I still remember Bishop Jones's topic that night, it was called "Break Out."

Bishop Jones's message inspired me. It gave me hope, but his sermon alone wasn't enough for me. Once the service was over, I noticed a table set up with Bishop Jones's products for sale. I wanted to purchase as much material as my pockets would allow. Although my back was turned, I overheard Bishop Jones near the table speaking to a group of young and upcoming ministers.

Meanwhile, I was having a great conversation with the sales rep at the table. I understood the biblical principle, "You have not, because you ask not."

So, while closing out my purchase, I said, "Can I write down a prayer request for you to give to Bishop to pray for me? Maybe if he has time on the plane..." She looked at me with a level of discernment and concern that went from sales rep to evangelist. It seemed like she could see the weight of pain I'd been carrying.

"I will get him right now," she said. And she walked

right over to him while he was engaged in conversation with the young ministers. He stopped what he was doing, turned and stepped over to me. I noticed that he was very tall.

He asked me about my prayer request. I told him all that I had been through with my brothers over the past month. You could tell my pain befell him and he had a great look of uneasiness. He was moved by the sincere look of hopelessness that was trying to consume me. Then, he looked me in the face, and his eyes began to swell up with tears.

"Nothing like that has ever happened to me. I'm very sorry to hear that," he said in his rasping voice. Then he grabbed me by the hands and prayed a short prayer over me. I received it. When he prayed for me, I didn't tell him my name, and we didn't exchange contact information, either. It was just prayer for that moment.

Many people attend church or hear a sermon and they'll say things like, "The preacher is preaching to me; how did he know what I was dealing with?" Shortly after Bishop prayed for me, I was watching his broadcast. He was showing some highlights, and during that broadcast, he made a statement in the most charismatic way he could. It was as if he knew I would be watching.

He said, "Your brother's death was for you to help somebody else's child stay alive!" He then yelled, "YOU GOT TO GO THROUGH IT!" Immediately when I heard that, I broke down in tears. I fell on my face and wept.

At that instant, I had an epiphany and said to myself, *That's it! I have to use my testimony to help other young people stay alive.*

DO SOMETHING WITH IT!

I used every last bit of energy and influence with a "stop the violence" mentality. I co-founded a not-for-profit organization called Men of Integrity, and traveled the country as an ambassador for YouthBuild while continuing to build with my team on YouthBuild's National Alumni Council.

For years, YouthBuild continued to send me all over the country. I continued to immerse myself in every opportunity I could. I spoke in panel discussions, facilitated trainings, and planned major conferences across the country. These were no small conferences, either. They lasted for days and hundreds attended. I specifically enjoyed delivering keynote speeches, hoping I made an impact with those in attendance.

For a while, I seemed to be living out of my suitcase and duffle bag. We were on the move and it was great! It seemed like I was always flying somewhere. Working for my local YouthBuild program gave me the freedom to be developed into a national leader. I had the opportunity to meet like-minded young people from other continents. We attended teachings and lectures on the topics of nonviolence and peace building strategies through the International Youth

Corp (IYC).

The IYC taught what it called the *Kingian* (Martin Luther King, Jr.) principles of nonviolence. I remember while traveling in the beautiful historic country of Israel, everyone in the group discussed pressing issues from their home countries. By doing so, we were able to get an idea of what people were facing around the world. We were taught that if our society was going to be a better place, it would be best to pour wisdom and knowledge in the youth of our world.

After everyone was able to speak on the issues affecting their countries, we'd then focus our attention on the issues affecting the country we were all visiting. Once the issues were put on the table, then the group would come up with our own ideas and solutions that could potentially get implemented.

Meanwhile, I had to say farewell to my services on the National Alumni Council (NAC). I ended almost a decade of service as President. There wasn't enough time and space to accomplish all that I had wanted. I needed to be sure that my work didn't continue to keep taking me from my family. I didn't want to tip the scales and give my children a father who put the outside world ahead of their growth and development. First and foremost, my family stayed at the head of my decisions. It was time for me to settle down. Val and I got married and we had more children together, which also meant I needed to cut back on some of my traveling.

The time came for me to pass the torch and serve in another capacity. I quickly shifted my priorities to making an impact in my own community. After all the things I learned through my experiences, it was time to come home and share.

SOLDIER

My phone started ringing off the hook. I didn't recognize the number, so I didn't answer it. It was July 27, 2013, and it was about 1:00 a.m. I was tired and figured it had to be a wrong number. It kept ringing, but it was a different number on my caller ID. I was a bit concerned, but it had stopped. As I grabbed my phone, it rang again and it was Aunt Loretta, which was really strange because she was in bed by seven or eight o'clock every night. I knew it had to be urgent for me to get a call from her that late.

I called her back and asked her what was going on.

"Ryan is dead."

I couldn't believe it. It couldn't be. He couldn't have died!

"Yes, he was murdered... Shot in the head," she said.

Even though Ryan and I had been off and on, he was still my best friend and everybody knew that. We were brothers, so even during our times apart, we still loved each other very much. I couldn't accept that he had been murdered. Before I woke Val up, I went to the restroom and wept for about fifteen minutes.

Val and I got dressed and went down to the hospital. By the time we got there, family and friends were scattered about, trying to figure out what happened. At the same time, stunned by disbelief and reality, shockwaves were sent through our hearts. I saw Grandma, trying to hold it together. I saw Ryan's dad and I began to cry and he joined me. Then I saw Ryan's sister, Erika. She was torn to shreds, but she escorted me to the operating room to view his body. I still couldn't believe that Ryan was gone. I saw his motionless body, and his head was wrapped in bandages where the bullet had penetrated. All I could hear was Erika telling me that he fought hard to stay alive. The doctors did all they could do to keep him alive, but the shot to the head was just too much for him.

When Ryan died, it felt like a part of my soul had been ripped away. He was my friend to the end, and I will miss him. He was a soldier! I've performed a lot of eulogies in my time, but his was by far the hardest one I had to endure.

MAKE THE MOVE

We may not have all shared the exact same life experiences when it comes to our upbringings, but knowing we have felt the irrefutable pain, that's what makes us kindred in spirit. Even though this writing was primarily about fatherlessness, the essence of this book applies to all who have been broken in one way or another.

If you are reading this book while you are incarcerated, it is imperative for you to focus. Read all you can read. Read so many books that the prison has to update its library. Come out of prison with understanding, knowledge, wisdom, vision and goals.

You may be reading this while you're locked up, and you may be thinking, *"Man, you don't know how hard it is for me up in here. My mother hasn't written me a letter in two years. None of my brothers or sisters ever come to see me, and my dad is nowhere to be found. None of my friends, except for my girlfriend who brings my kids, visit me either. I hardly ever have money on my books to purchase my basic needs. I have to survive up in here and that means I have to do what I have to do until my time is served. In fact, Mr. Mike Dean, how can you tell me anything when you haven't been in my shoes? I'm going to need you to shut up with all of that 'reading books' stuff. I need money, and I need it now. And when I get out, I'm going right back to where I left off... back to hanging with my old friends. They tell me when I get out, they are going to throw me a big party and everybody is going to be there. Once they finish taking me out, they are going to buy me clothes and put money in my pocket. So for real-for real, I hear you, but I can't feel you."*

To all of my brothers and sisters who are locked up and

thinking like that, you are on the verge of being "recycled." That kind of thinking is a systematic trap. In fact, Dr. Myles Munroe said, "Show me your friend and I will show you your future."

On the other hand, you may be locked up, thinking, *"Okay, Mr. Mike Dean. I'm hearing you and I can feel everything you are saying. But, what do you do when you don't have anybody? I don't have any support when I get out of prison, let alone any support while I'm behind these walls."*

Trust me, I wish I had all of the answers. I will say this: you must have a vision and a step-by-step plan if you want to stay out of prison and achieve success. You must also list your relational assets and liabilities, meaning you must assess the people you will contact who will help keep you out of prison. I can guarantee that the moment you are free, somebody is going to try to get you involved in the wrong things. As much as I'm not a fan of the way our prison system recidivates people, I do agree that there are people who genuinely need to be incarcerated, nonetheless.

I am not minimizing crime and punishment by any means. But anyone who has been incarcerated has been plucked out of his life and has been forced to live a life that has been created for him. This takes time to get used to physically, mentally and emotionally.

Most prisons provide dorms, large open rooms like warehouses that fit in as many bunk beds as they can squeeze. Inmates suddenly share furniture in a three-and-a-half foot space with someone they didn't choose. All the inmates' possessions are tucked in metal lockboxes and hiding places, but their small space still can be invaded by C.O.s or other inmates trying to steal. Everything is watched, and if inmates cry out as a result of injustice, they may be silenced by some type of punishment until they learn how to "shut up and take it" the best way they can. Curfews and mealtimes are enforced and non-participation is not an option.

I remember having a conversation with a family member who served five years. He said, *"Man, y'all don't know how it is in there. I have to play basketball wearing pants and a long-sleeve shirt, not to mention something to cover my neck. People who have diseases are not treated in here at all. In fact, they are put in general population with everyone else and I can't risk being scratched by someone with a deadly disease."*

That statement blew my mind. I would have never thought that things like that go on behind the walls of prisons. I assumed that gangs and other criminal activities were typical in institutions, but I never imagined the level of neglect that inmates endure. I wonder how many people who are incarcerated develop mental illnesses while behind the walls? After serving three-to-five years, some ex-offenders experienced changes and habits that seemed to happen without their permission, shifting their thinking forever.

I firmly believe that if you do the crime, you do the time. But, often people are given time that doesn't seem to fit the crime. I knew men who were locked up for multiple years as a result of a few rocks of crack. These were people who were trying to feed their families a good meal and maybe provide them with a few wants. These were people who were trying to achieve "The American Dream" the only way they knew how. For society to see real change, we must remember that we are dealing with human beings, not animals. Everyone has made mistakes, and everyone deserves to be treated with dignity.

Unfortunately, the trend seems to show that ex-offenders stay imprisoned in society even after they are free.

After serving time in prison, the ex-offender may return home with a new mindset: "I'm a changed man! I am going to do something different with my life. I'm going to settle down, find a job, take care of my kids, and stay out of trouble."

But once a person gets out of prison, that person's opportunity to go to college or get a job has been branded with a scarlet letter that says, "time served." Not only were laws created to keep ex-offenders out of mainstream America, but many companies even have set rules and requirements to keep ex-offenders out of their organizations. And if an ex-offender can get a job with a reputable company, there is no guarantee for success or advancement in that particular organization. Ex-offenders often can't even earn recognized certifications or degrees because of their record. Unless the ex-offender is connected to the right people who can help him into a position of growth, success is not in his favor. He may not even have a clue that he is already in the circle of "recycle," and if he is not focused, eventually he will find himself incarcerated again.

In fact, the people I know who came home from prison "rehabilitation centers" had more knowledge about criminal activity than they did before they went in. It was like they went into prison with a criminal bachelor's degree, and came out with a Ph.D. Plus, they were isolated so long from a world that constantly evolves technologically. Any type of training they received, or resources they used behind the gates, would have been outdated at least by ten years.

As a result, many offenders come out of prison thinking they are ready to enter society, but many are not as ready as they think. Assimilation to society is difficult as it is, and often people come out of prison with major trust issues as well. Those trust issues limit progress and create a constant mental fight. When the mental fight gets tough, it's easy to lean back on familiar habits of the past: drug abuse, violence and crime–thus the cycle of "recycle."

Imagine the difference in the success of an ex-offender if his circumstances were ideal right from his release. Imagine the ex-offender's success if on his first day back into society, his driver's license was reinstated and he had an affordable place to stay, including six months of food stamps until he was able to stand alone.

No organism can survive such abrupt changes to its surroundings without being damaged. Even when someone buys a small fish from a pet store, great care is taken to protect its little life. The fish is bagged in a Ziploc bag filled with water kept at the right temperature for the fish to remain alive. The seller further instructs the buyer to prep his home fish tank first to ensure the right temperature and free it from all toxins. Once the environment is ideal, the buyer should put the fish (still enclosed in the bag in which it was purchased) in the tank. When the temperature of the bag and tank balance out, only then can the fish be released into its new surroundings. If the fish abruptly entered a new tank of water ill-prepared, it would die of shock.

It's very difficult to service offenders and ex-offenders when most services are based on theory. Further, many people genuinely want to help the prison population without fully understanding the real needs. Proverbs 4:7 (NKJV) says, "Wisdom is the principal thing; Therefore get wisdom. And in all your getting, get understanding." Understanding the needs of this population is part of the battle, but not the answer to the war.

Fathers, do not wait. You must make the move to affirm your child. If you don't, your absence will inevitably affect generations to come. I know this because it affected my family. I went to school with a cousin, not knowing at all that we were related. In fact, although he and I didn't hang out, we had respect for each other. Imagine if we would have known we were cousins. Imagine the family support we could have given each other along the way. It's very likely that we would have spent more time with each other. I would have been part of family cookouts and reunions.

Wonder hasn't let go of me. Maybe I wonder too much. Maybe you wonder, too, while you are reading this book on your break or while the clothes are washing and the kids are off to school. You might not fully admit it to yourself, but you want your daddy. I spent most of my life wondering how my journey would have been different if I would have had my father. But maybe being fatherless was meant to be. Maybe I had to grow up without my dad so that I could spark a movement of fathers marching on Capitol Hill. Maybe my pain of abandonment was my call to encourage fathers from all classes, races and religions to march back into the homes of their families.

Having children of my own gave me a whole new insight on why fathers should be in the lives of their children. As a father, I had to decide that I wanted to be a part of their lives. I never read a step-by-step manual on how to be a father. Hard knocks had become my middle name. I understood that ultimately I only had one life to live. So I thought about all the things I had wanted from my father, and that is how I "fathered" my family. The first thing I did was make sure that I was there–that I was present.

Val and I have four beautiful girls, along with full custody of my handsome nephew. There will never be enough pages in any book to describe the love I feel for my family. I wouldn't trade being there for my children for all the riches of the world. It is incredible when your child jumps in your lap and kisses you on the cheek. It is truly amazing to watch your child slowly fight going to sleep while exhaustion from playtime wins the battle and lures her into a dream. And as soon as I walk into the house every day after work, I'm greeted by my babies who yell almost simultaneously, "DADDY!" Hearing their little voices in harmony makes me feel like the greatest man in the universe. They know my walk and they know my smell. They know that when they need me, I'll be there. I am their superhero.

How you treat yourself will conclusively determine the quality of your existence, too. It's your life and you have to take full advantage of your gifts. You have the choice to be present, relevant and important in your children's lives. You are not an afterthought and neither are they. Your children want you. They need you. Today. Now.

"Daddy, it's been rough without you," your child will say. "But, I love you."

"Faith is taking the first step even
when you can't see the whole staircase."
~Martin Luther King, Jr.

EPILOGUE

"Never apply a permanent solution
to a temporary problem."
~Dr. Myles Munroe

As a kid, one of my favorite summer activities was community water fights. We didn't need water guns or water hoses, and most of us in the hood couldn't afford those things anyway. Instead, each family filled pots, pans, cups, jugs or buckets with water. The object was to catch somebody unaware and pour water on them. Everyone was involved, which made it so much fun. This was not just a kid thing. Toddlers, grandfathers and everyone in between ran around chasing people with cups and sometimes by the time they faced their opponent, the cup was empty. Although our community had been slammed with poverty and turmoil, we insisted on creating ways to share enjoyable moments with

237

one another. Those were the moments when we forgot about the gruesome challenges of everyday life.

Life told us that we were being deprived of living out our childhoods. Life forced us to learn to make adult decisions as kids. Society told us that being a low-income family forced us to miss out on memorable moments. But those community water fights proved otherwise. On those hot days as well as in life, I had to keep my head up, even when I thought the water was too deep for me to stand.

Former Principal of YouthBuild Columbus Community School Derek Steward said, "Failure leads to success." I soon came to grips with the fact that although I failed, that didn't make me a failure. Just like in the park when D-Train shoved me to the ground, I got up and dusted myself off. I did the same thing throughout my life when I made a mistake—I always got up and dusted myself off. Sometimes I didn't want to get up. But the longer I stayed down, the more I knew I didn't belong there.

I remember the day when one of my mother's friends asked if could he use my bike—the BMX bike I got for Christmas while living with Uncle Shug. He had a devious look in his eye when he asked me. He said he just wanted to ride to the store and he would be right back. I had a bad feeling in my gut, but my mom made me let him ride my bike to the store. I was angry, and I waited for hours on the porch for him to return with my bike. He never came back. Days went by, and I waited and looked around the neighborhood for my bike. I asked everyone, but no one had seen it or the man who took it. My mom even looked for him. But he was gone.

If I had never had a bike, I never would have missed it so much when it was taken from me. That's how I felt when I lost my mother and my brother. That's how I felt when I lost Ryan. Meeting my father was like that, too.

Dealing with problems led me to develop a level of immunity toward things I couldn't control. If I didn't create some level of mental resistance, then my problems would have held me hostage. I had to make necessary adjustments and refocus myself. I never got used to coping with pain, but I did learn to mask it. I became a Masters of the Mask.

I know life is hard. I know how comfortable it is behind the mask. But one thing that got me through those tough times was the knowledge that someone else out there had it worse than I did and he made it through. It is my hope that my story encourages you to see that you can make it through, too.

Your reality says, "I've been trying my hardest to live right. But trying to live off of minimum wage is impossible and I need to take care of my family. I work many days and long hours just to barely make ends meet."

Trust me when I tell you this: the right thing to do is say "NO" to the street life. Your life is bigger and more important than crime and violence. Your life is more than bling and hype. You have purpose in you to do something great. Do yourself and those around you a favor: do not get into the street life. If you're already involved in that life, get out while you can.

You may be reading this book in your library, on a plane, on your porch or from your prison cell. You may have read this whole book and still want to continue that street life. I've heard lots of people say, "That's all I know." That's their only rationale: continuing to do what's familiar to them. You may think *that's all you know,* but it doesn't mean that's all you can learn. Be smart and take advantage of change while change is still a viable option.

When I was cooking crack on my stove, I had no idea that I would later speak on FOX Television News on the issues of violence in Black America. I had no idea that my presence would be requested years later by the planning committee of the 2007 Congressional Black Caucus in Washington, D.C. When I was being taken out by S.W.A.T., I had no idea that I would ever leave that life and later share with politicians my views on being young, gifted and Black in America.

To this day, I'm still connected with most of the staff from when I first got involved in YouthBuild. I had the opportunity to be a speaker at the *Aspen Ideas Festival*, and it was there that I had the honor and privilege to present on a panel. We discussed living in low-income communities and shared our stories of transformation to an influential group of people including Colin Powell and his wife. Jamie Dimon was also in attendance. After the panel, Mr. Dimon and I had a brief conversation. I said to him, "Mr. Dimon as a successful businessman such as yourself, what advice would you give someone up and coming like myself?" His answer was simple:

"Whatever you do, DON'T GIVE UP."

I served on the NAC for eight years and each year I grew in wisdom and in stature throughout the YouthBuild movement. For seven of those years, I served on the Executive Committee. By the time my NAC years were finished, I had served one term as President.

The majority of my time on the NAC was spent with Alicia Mckinney, Jamie Turner and Antonio Ramirez (a.k.a. the "Dream Team"). We helped to revolutionize the NAC through business and organizational methods. This group became my inner circle. Dr. Eugene Lundy often said, "Teamwork makes the dream work." We did whatever we had to do to take things to the next level, even if that meant being on conference calls during the wee hours of the night or traveling to Jamie's place in Indianapolis for the weekend. We supported each other through our ups and downs. That is a family—a set of lifelong relationships which can't be broken.

Alongside my work with NAC and YouthBuild, I spent

three years as director of the teenage and young adult ministries at a local church. And I knew in my heart that one day I'd become a pastor. It was then that I moved under the leadership of my uncle, who taught me how his own ministry operated. I also learned how to build relationships with parishioners and I learned how to build a church facility from the ground up. But the call within me to become a pastor kept growing stronger. I chose to trust God and start my own church, which I believe was God's original intent for my life. As I transitioned, I was treated very well and was regarded with high esteem. In fact, I had the privilege of leading a team of fellow leaders. They are family, and at times I really miss the times we shared doing outreach trainings and helping to build the organization.

God pushed me out of the eagle's nest to put me in position to lead. So I chose to lead in the community where I grew up: the Arms. To cut costs, a member of the "Dream Team" donated our flyer design. We even advertised free hotdogs and hamburgers following the service. I didn't have a band or singers, and we didn't have ushers or greeters. Instead, we borrowed a complicated sound system from a guy who willingly donated his equipment to us until we were able to afford our own. I rented a room at the recreation center on Sundays and Wednesdays and we paid five hundred dollars per month for that, which was very affordable. We started out with only two families as church members. Later, services drew almost 250 people with my sermon title, "I FEEL YOUR PAIN." Today, the family of Power City Church continues to grow.

I spent years believing that a crew in the hood was my family. And I could have stayed there, leaning on the "that's all I know" mentality. So, here's what I say to a generation that believes that what they see in the moment is "all they know:"

Embrace positive change and hold tight to your true family.

Even though change is scary and unfamiliar, change in the right direction leads to growth. It's just like the anxiety of getting ready to have a baby. When Ryan's girlfriend and my girlfriend were both pregnant at the same time, Ryan and I soon discovered the challenges of trying to prepare for something we knew nothing about. Then reality smashed us right in the face like a cream pie. We realized that our lives weren't just about us anymore. That's when we vowed to always be there for our children and to love, teach, and guide them in their futures. I realized that I was in a relationship for life, whether or not Val and I stayed together. I wasn't going to let anyone or anything stop me from being in my child's life. Little did I know that Val and I would later marry and produce four beautiful girls.

That's when I understood more about real fatherhood. I remember watching Angie's father come get her at all hours of the night. I can understand his actions now that I have four daughters of my own. Just maybe God is showing me how Angie's father must have felt. I can't imagine being in his shoes.

I also can't help wondering how Ryan's life would have been different if his father would have visited his children more often. Since then, I've witnessed many cases where the father left and never looked back, regardless of the cry of his child. The child waves from his bedroom window, expecting his father to turn and wave back before he drives off. How disappointing when that child doesn't get a wave back! I have to ask another question to the fathers: why didn't you at least look back?

Questions for parents:
- What dangers do your children face while living with you?
- Can you see the instability in your child's life?
- Do you know what's going on in the home where your child lives?
- What are you doing to help support your child(ren)? How can you support them more?
- How often are you visiting?
- How often do you look for changes in behavior?
- Do your children trust you enough to consult with you about the happenings in their lives?

Right now, your daughter is in her dorm room working on her finals, and she wishes she had her father to help her. She needs you there to tell her about guys and how she needs to be careful about falling for the wrong one. Your daughter may be trying to get her car fixed and the repair shop is trying to take advantage of her inexperience. She needs you!

Look at your six-year-old son. He doesn't have a clue how to fix the popped chain on his bike. Your son is tired of looking up at the bleachers during a game and not seeing Daddy in the crowd. He needs you!

They need you, but first you have to know that you are needed. And you have to want to be there to fulfill their precious need.

Go get her! Go get him! Your son needs you—he's locked up in prison. Go get your girl—she needs you. Your grandkids need you. They need your presence. YOU ARE NEEDED!

Write them, send them pictures of you, pay your child support and take them with you. Spend time with them on "normal" days, not just on special occasions. Every moment with your child is a special occasion. When you are wrong, apologize with your heart and then move forward one day at a time. If your child has never seen you in his life, then you may feel like a stranger. Still, that never changes the fact that the child is YOURS.

I believe that fathers should be involved in their children's lives because they genuinely care, not just because it is court ordered. Regardless of their family background or their level of success, fathers instill valuable things in their children—mannerisms, morals, and ethical and spiritual beliefs. No matter what your child's physical situation, you as a father must find it in your heart to finish what you started.

ABOUT THE AUTHOR
MIKE DEAN

MIKE DEAN, a native of Columbus, Ohio, is the Director of Franklin County YouthBuild, an affiliate of YouthBuild USA, a national non-profit organization whose mission is to "unleash the intelligence and positive energy of low-income youth to rebuild their lives." Dean is also a successful entrepreneur and founder and pastor of Power City Church, an Ohio based ministry.

Dean is the former President of the National Alumni Council (NAC), which is the governing body of the YouthBuild USA National Alumni Association. In this capacity, Mike provided leadership to more than 100,000 young Americans throughout the United States.

A sought-after national lecturer and youth advocate, Dean is also a member of the Graduate Speakers Bureau. As a powerful advocate for disenfranchised youth across America, Mike Dean has traveled to Capitol Hill to address the U.S. Congress, among other engagements. Most notably, Mike addressed the prestigious 2007 Congressional Black Caucus in Washington, D.C. where he shared his views at length on being young, gifted, and black in America. In

2008, Mike presented at the Youth Service Conference in Orlando, Florida and the Aspen Ideas Festival in Aspen, Colorado. He has also been a guest on numerous radio and television shows.

Dean hosts an internet radio talk show called "Holla @ me!" where he primarily deals with the issue of fatherlessness and relevant topics facing our society.

Learn more about Mike at **DeanBooks.com**.